The Motor Trade &
The Affections of May

Lee. J. Campbell (l) and John Dolan (r), Theatre New Brunswick.

Playwrights Canada Press is the publishing imprint of
the Playwrights Union of Canada: 54 Wolseley St., 2nd fl.
Toronto, Ontario CANADAM5T 1A5
Tel. (416) 947-0201 Fax. (416) 947-0159

Playwrights Canada Press operates with the generous assistance of
The Canada Council - Writing and Publishing Section, and Theatre
Section, and the Ontario Arts Council.

*Front cover: Catherine Barroll & Ron Gabriel, Theatre New
Brunswick, Fredericton, 1990. Photos by Dale McBride.
Edited and designed by Tony Hamill.*

Canadian Cataloguing in Publication Data
Norm Foster, 1949 —
        The motor trade: and, The affections of May
Plays
ISBN 0-88754-491-6
I. Title. II. Title: the affections of May.
PS8561.077M6   1993   C812'.54   C93-094734-7
PR9199.3.F67M6   1993

First edition: August 1993
Printed and bound in Winnipeg, Manitoba, Canada.

To Janet

Thank you to Michael Shamata whose input into both of these plays was invaluable.

- Norm Foster

Table of Contents

The Motor Trade was first produced by Theatre New Brunswick in Fredericton, 1991, in association with Theatre Calgary with the following cast:

PHIL	*Lee J. Campbell*
DAN	*John Dolan*
GAIL	*Catherine Barroll*
DARLENE	*Laurie Paton*

Directed by Michael Shamata.
Designed by Patrick Clark.
Lighting by Harry Frehner.
Stage manager - Sandra McEwing.

The Motor Trade was subsequently produced by Theatre Aquarius, Hamilton, 1993 with the following cast:

PHIL	*Wayne Best*
DAN	*Ronn Sarosiak*
GAIL	*Mary Long*
DARLENE	*Shannon Lawson*

Directed by Peter Mandia.
Designed by Maxine Graham.
Lighting by James Milburn.
Stage manager - Stephen Newman.

THE CHARACTERS

PHIL MOSS
Forty-five years old. Has worked in automobile sales for most of his adult life. Owns a small dealership with his partner Dan Torelli.

DAN TORELLI
Forty-two years old. Has decided that it's time to get out of the automotive trade.

DARLENE MOSS
Phil's wife.

GAIL PIERCE
Revenue Canada Employee.

Act One, Scene One

The time is the present. A stormy winter's day. The play takes place in the showroom of Doral Valley Motors, a car dealership owned by Phil Moss and Dan Torelli. It's not a big showroom, not big enough to accommodate a car. In the showroom are three desks. Phil's desk is D.R., Dan's desk is D.L. and Ted's desk is U.L. In front of each of the three desks is a chair or two for the customers to sit in when they are closing their car deals. Phil and Dan each have their own file cabinets near their desks. U.C. is a table with a coffee maker, styrofoam cups and coffee fixings on it. Under the table is a small icebox. Next to this table is a sofa or bench for customers to sit on and a coffee table with magazines on it. On the walls are posters of new cars. S.R. is the entrance to the showroom. There is a coat rack just inside this door. S.L. is an exit to the washroom and another exit to a room used as the boardroom. D.C. is the imaginary showroom window which looks out onto the car lot and also out to the strip joint across the street.

As the scene opens, PHIL and DAN are on stage. DAN sits at his desk reading the newspaper and sipping a coffee while PHIL stands D.C. and looks out the showroom window toward the audience. They both wear suits. PHIL has an unlit cigarette in his hand. He unwraps a stick of gum and puts it into his mouth.

PHIL   Goddamn snow. Will ya look at the goddamn snow? I've never seen so much goddamn snow. Goddamn. We're not gonna move much iron today, Danny. No sir.

DAN	(*not really listening*) You don't think so?
PHIL	Well, take a look. You ever seen so much goddamn snow?
DAN	(*still reading*) No, I guess not.
PHIL	I guess not. Who's gonna go shopping for a car in weather like this? And on a Saturday too. Our best day. Damn. Even our salesman isn't showing up for godssake. Huh? It's ten thirty and where is he? (*taking out a comb and combing his hair*)
DAN	Hmm?
PHIL	Ted. Where the hell is he?
DAN	I don't know.
PHIL	He hasn't even called.
DAN	Probably stuck in the snow.
PHIL	Well, of course he is. Look at the goddamn stuff. I've never seen so much goddamn snow. I was in Greenland once they didn't have this much snow.

> *The phone on PHIL's desk buzzes and he answers it.*

Doral Valley Motors, Phil Moss...Yessir. Uh-huh. You were in when? Tuesday. And what were you looking at sir?...The Pontiac. Well, which Pontiac, sir. We've got about a dozen Pontiacs on the lot right now...The Pontiac LTD. That's a Ford, sir...Yes. Honest mistake. Yessir, I remember you now. Yes... you're not sure what the price was? Well, lemme check it for you. (*rustling some papers on his desk without looking at them*) Uh...Twelve five, sir...Beg your pardon? Eleven three? Hang on. (*rustling more paper*) Yessir, you're absolutely right. It is eleven three. My mistake. I was looking at an

PHIL

(*continued*) old price list...Right...Warranty? Yessir, that comes with the famous Doral Valley 'curb and gutter' warranty. (*covering the mouthpiece of the phone and speaking to DAN*) Once it's over the curb, you got her. (*back to the phone*) Yessir...Uh-huh. We sure do. What kind of car would you like to trade in? A '79 Chevette. How much could we give you for it? Well, that depends, sir. How much gas is in it?...Look, I'll tell you what. Why don't you come in on Monday and we'll talk? Right. We'll look forward to seeing you sir. You bet. Bye-bye.

> *PHIL hangs up and moves to the table to pour himself a cup of coffee.*

Well, at least the day isn't gonna be a total loss. Guy's a walkover. He was in Tuesday looking at the '86 LTD. I quoted him eleven three and he didn't even try to talk me down to a skinnier deal. We should just throw him out front there and use him for a welcome mat. You want another coffee?

DAN

No thanks.

PHIL

Donut?

DAN

No.

PHIL

God, ever since I quit smoking, all I do is put stuff in my mouth. Gum, coffee, donuts. I can't get enough.

DAN

It's oral gratification.

PHIL

Hmm?

DAN

That's what it's called. Oral gratification.

PHIL

Hey, I'm just talkin' about coffee and donuts here.

DAN	That's what oral gratification is. You're satisfying your need for a cigarette by putting other things in your mouth.
PHIL	(*after a beat, at the refrigerator*) Yeah, but just coffee and donuts.
DAN	Right.
PHIL	Right. (*taking a bite of a donut*) You think I'm putting on weight?
DAN	Who you?
PHIL	Yeah, what do you think? Can you notice it?
DAN	Naw.
PHIL	You sure?
DAN	A pound or two maybe. It's nothing.
PHIL	That's what happens when you quit smoking. You gain weight.
DAN	Greenland? When were you in Greenland?
PHIL	What?
DAN	You said you were in Greenland.
PHIL	Yeah. Last year when I was in England. You remember.
DAN	That was England. That wasn't Greenland.
PHIL	Yeah, but on the way back the plane had engine trouble and we had to put down in Greenland. You remember that.
DAN	Greenland?
PHIL	Yeah.

DAN	I thought it was Iceland.
PHIL	No, it was Greenland.
DAN	I thought you told me Iceland.
PHIL	No.
DAN	I mean, Greenland's not even on the way is it?
PHIL	Well, that's where we put down.
DAN	No, your flight path would probably take you over Iceland then Newfoundland. I don't think you'd go anywhere near Greenland. You sure it wasn't Iceland?
PHIL	Hey, what am I, Charles-fucking-Lindberg? It was cold and there was snow. Figure it out.
DAN	It was probably Iceland. I mean, Greenland's up there too, but you'd probably miss Greenland altogether.
PHIL	Fine. All I'm saying, Mr. Rand McNally, is that there was a lot of snow wherever the hell it was, all right?
DAN	(*still reading his newspaper*) Probably Iceland.
	DAN's phone buzzes and he answers it .
DAN	Doral Valley Motors Yeah, Ted Yeah, I know. Is it what? (*hand over phone, to PHIL*) Guy lives half a mile away and he wants to know if it's snowing here too...(*back to phone*)
PHIL	(*leaning into the phone*) No, Ted, it's sunny and warm here, ya goddamned idiot!
DAN	Yeah, that was Phil. Uh-huh...Right. Okay, whenever you can make it. We'll see ya. (*to PHIL*) He's shovelling his car out. Says he'll be here as soon as he can.

DAN goes back to his paper.

PHIL   (*moving down with his coffee*) Yeah, he's probably usin' the snow as an excuse to jump the ol' skin train one more time.

DAN   Who, Ted?

PHIL   Sure. Him and the wife? 'All aboard'!

DAN   No, I don't think so. Ted's pretty conscientious. If he could get here, he'd get here.

PHIL   Hey, I'm conscientious too. Doesn't mean I don't like to get the ol' lug nuts tightened once in a while. God, I'll tell you what I'd like right now. A cigarette. This is the toughest time you know. With that coffee in the morning? I mean, a cigarette with your morning coffee is better than sex.

DAN   You must be having sex with the wrong women.

PHIL   Hey, at least I'm having it. Of course, you know what they say. Sex is like Bridge. If you don't have a good partner you'd better have a good hand. Well, you'd know all about that, wouldn't you? Huh?

DAN   Thank you.

PHIL   Well, I mean, good God. I don't know how you do it, Dan. I honest to Christ don't.

DAN   Don't get started, Phil, all right?

PHIL   Well, really now, when was the last time you had your ticket punched?

DAN   What?

PHIL   Come on, when?

DAN   What's it to you?

PHIL   I'm worried about you. A man goes that long
        without it, it's not normal. I mean, if it was me,
        I'd be looking twice at well-groomed sheep dogs
        by now.

DAN   Well, it's not you, so try and get over it.

PHIL   Well, I feel like I have to look out for you, you
        know?

DAN   Well, you don't.

PHIL   I could set you up if you want.

DAN   No thanks.

PHIL   You don't want me to?

DAN   No.

PHIL   Okay, but I know a divorced mother of three,
        drives a loaded Le Mans, gets a fat alimony check
        every month, and she's into motorized
        implements, you know what I'm sayin'?

DAN   Gee, and she hasn't been snapped up yet?

PHIL   Fine. Make fun. But, don't say I didn't offer.
        (*beat*) Hey, I'm using a new aftershave today. Did
        you notice?

DAN   No.

PHIL   Yeah. Ten years an Old Spice man, today Mr.
        Ice-Blue Aqua Velva. (*moving to DAN*) Take a
        whiff and see what you think. (*leaning over to
        DAN*)

DAN   Not bad.

PHIL   So, tell me the truth. If you're a woman, and you
        smell this on me, you're gonna want to jump
        me, right?

DAN	Oh, come on.
PHIL	No, tell me.
DAN	Get out.
PHIL	Come on.
DAN	I can't answer that.
PHIL	Why not?
DAN	Because I've always wanted to jump you.
PHIL	You see what I've been telling you? You've been without it for too long. (*looking out the window*) God, look at it out there.
DAN	(*looking out*) Yeah, she's comin' down all right. (*back to his paper*)
PHIL	You know why I hate the snow? Huh? It reminds me of hockey.
DAN	I thought you liked hockey.
PHIL	I love it. Are you kiddin'? You know that. That's why I hate the snow. Every time I see snow it reminds me that I never made it as a pro hockey player.
DAN	You wanted to be a hockey player?
PHIL	Ever since I was five.
DAN	So, what happened?
PHIL	Couldn't skate.
DAN	(*beat*) Yeah, that'd do it. (*back to his paper*)

PHIL	Goddamn ankles. I've always had weak ankles. My old man, he used to build a rink in the back yard every winter, and he'd get me out there trying to teach me how to skate, and I'd be walkin' around the ice on my ankles. Every year from the time I was about three until I was ten he had me out there. First he'd buy me ankle supports, then he'd tape my ankles inside the ankle supports, then he bought me a pair of skates with built-in ankle supports, and he put the store-bought ankle supports inside of those and taped my ankles inside of those. Nothin' worked. I must've owned - what - five, six pair of skates in my life. Never once had to get them sharpened. I still love the game though. God. The Leafs, huh? Back in the sixties? What a team. Jesus, they were a team. Mahovlich. Keon. Hey, come on, college boy. Give me a number and I'll give you the player.
DAN	What?
PHIL	A number. Give me a number.
DAN	(*still reading his paper.*) Ten.
PHIL	George Armstrong. Gimme another.
DAN	Twelve.
PHIL	Ron Stewart. Another.
DAN	Four.
PHIL	Red Kelly. One more.
DAN	Twenty-one.
PHIL	Bobby Baun. Come on, give me a tough one.
DAN	Phil...
PHIL	Come on.

DAN	How do I know what a tough one is?
PHIL	A tough one is...nineteen.
DAN	Nineteen.
PHIL	Kent Douglas. Huh? Now, that's a tough one. Man, what a team that was. Bob Pulford. Dickie Duff. You ever play hockey?
DAN	When I was a kid, sure.
PHIL	Were you any good?
DAN	Well, I used to get my skates sharpened once in a while if that's what you mean.
PHIL	It's a great game, isn't it? It's a lot like life when you think about it. You're out there bumpin' heads with a bunch of people you don't like, gettin' knocked on your ass, pickin' yourself up again —
DAN	(*reading the paper*) Oh, God.
PHIL	What?
DAN	Here's Jerry's obituary.
PHIL	Oh, no.
DAN	(*reading*) Henderson, Jerry. Suddenly at his home on Thursday, January 23rd.
PHIL	The poor bastard. He was one of the best, you know that?
DAN	Beloved husband of Mary. Dear father of Lois and Nestor.
PHIL	Nestor. Why in the hell would Jerry do that? Name his kid Nestor. I never understood that.
DAN	It was Jerry's grandfather's name.

PHIL	Oh, but still. Good God. Nestor.
DAN	Resting at the Goodfellow Funeral home. Funeral Sunday, eleven a.m., at the Franklin Cemetery.
PHIL	Good luck in this weather. They're gonna have to drag him up there behind a goddamned ski-doo.
DAN	That's all it says.
PHIL	Hmm?
DAN	That's all it says. They mention his family and his funeral.
PHIL	So, what do you want them to say?
DAN	Well, they should say something about *him*.
PHIL	Like what?
DAN	I don't know. Something that tells you what kind of a guy he was.
PHIL	He was the kind of guy who liked spanking his secretary with a ping pong paddle? You want that in there?
DAN	No, I mean...well, they should say what he did with his life.
PHIL	And what was that?
DAN	Well, he... Jesus, he ran that dealership for thirty-five years. Doesn't that count for anything?
PHIL	He was a car salesman, Dan. He wasn't Ghandi.
DAN	That shouldn't matter.
PHIL	Do you remember that?

DAN   What?

PHIL   The time we walked into his office unannounced
                 and he had whats-her-name across his knee? What
                 was her name? Terry...Terry something. And he's
                 got her across his knee, her skirt hiked up, ping
                 pong paddle up in the air and in we walk.
                 (*laughing now*) And there they are, both of them
                 just staring at us in shock. And Jerry says...he
                 says a spider went up her skirt and he was killing
                 it for her. And you say...you say "Damn, I guess
                 that means we're in for some rain now."
                 (*laughing uncontrollably now*)

DAN   (*laughing a little too*) Come on, Phil. The man's
                 dead. Have a little respect. (*laughing more*)
                 Spider.

PHIL   Oh, God. Stupid bastard. Don't get me wrong
                 though. I loved Jerry. You know that. I loved the
                 guy. I wonder what ever happened to her. Great
                 legs.

DAN   (*laughter subsiding*) It's still not right though.

PHIL   What isn't?

DAN   A man dies and the only thing they remember
                 about him is that he had a wife and two kids.

PHIL   Come on, Dan. What else did he do? He ran a car
                 dealership —

DAN   Well, that's what *we* do. Isn't that anything?

PHIL   Sure it is but...

DAN   Well, why can't they put it down? Owned
                 Henderson Motors. Just put that down.

PHIL   Danny, it's the family that writes these things
                 up. I mean, if they thought his being in the
                 motor trade was important, they would've put it
                 down.

DAN	What, you think they didn't think it was important?
PHIL	Well, how the hell should I know? I'll tell you this much though. If I'm his son, and I got a name like Nestor, I'm not even goin' to the funeral.
DAN	(*almost to himself, looking at paper*) They shoulda said more than this.
PHIL	Yeah, well, nothing you can do about it now. Man, I sure owe him a lot. We both do, huh? I meant he hired me when I was goin' nowhere. I had no experience, nothin'. Jerry taught me everything about this business. And then he loans us the money to buy this place. Guy was a saint. (*looking out of the window*) Will you look at that? We've got a blizzard outside and the strip joint across the street is packed. Look at it. The lot's full. Now, explain that to me. I mean, in the first place, who wants to watch strippers at ten-thirty in the morning, huh? I mean, the woman's up there shakin' it with the Tim Horton's coffee in her hand. She's half awake for Chrissake. What the hell's the attraction? Jesus. (*taking a sip of coffee*) You wanna go over?
DAN	It's not important, is it?
PHIL	What?
DAN	What we do. Selling cars.
PHIL	Sure it is. Goods and services, pal. The country runs on that shit.
DAN	But, in the overall scheme of things...the big picture...it's not that important, is it?
PHIL	Big picture. You wanna know what the big picture is? You're born, you work your ass off, you die, you're forgotten. That's the big picture.

	my friend. (*throwing his chewing gum in the waste basket*) God I hate this stuff. You got any Chiclets?
DAN	I wonder if they were ashamed of what he did for a living. His kids I mean.
PHIL	Ah, kids. What do they know? Ungrateful little bastards. How're yours doin' anyway?
DAN	Hmm? Oh, great. Great. Kristy's really enjoying law school, and Matt's...well, Matt's Matt, you know?
PHIL	Yeah, he's a good kid. What is he, eighteen now?
DAN	Nineteen.
PHIL	Nineteen. Still workin' over at the travel agency?
DAN	Uh-huh.
PHIL	Been there almost a year now, hasn't he?
DAN	Almost.
PHIL	Yeah, I figured. (*beat*) He's not gay, is he?
DAN	What? No. Matt?
PHIL	Well, it's just that Tom Baker's kid, what's-his-name, Donnie, used to work over there and he's gay.
DAN	So what, you think they only hire gays?
PHIL	Well, either that or maybe after you work there for a while you turn into one.
DAN	Get off.
PHIL	What's the matter?
DAN	Turn into one?

PHIL	Sure. It's like all convenience store owners are Oriental. It's the same thing. I've got a theory about that. It's like *Invasion of the Body Snatchers.* You buy a convenience store and somebody comes to your house and leaves one of these pods. You wake up the next morning, you're Oriental. Same with car salesmen. We're all white. Ever noticed that? Huh? Sure. Oriental guy buys a car dealership, he wakes up the next morning, he's white, fifteen pounds overweight and got a blond wife named Mitzi. Think about it.
DAN	You know what you are, Phil? You're a racist.
PHIL	What, racist.
DAN	You are. And you perpetuate stereotypes.
PHIL	Get out.
DAN	You do. You probably think all male hairdressers are gay too.
PHIL	*(after a beat, as if it's a given)* So?
DAN	You see? See what I mean?
PHIL	Hey, don't be so naive, Danny. You've got no idea what's going on out there these days.
DAN	Oh, and you do, I suppose.
PHIL	I know what I know. And don't go calling me a racist.
DAN	Well, what would you call it?
PHIL	I'm an observer. An astute observer, all right?
DAN	An observer.

PHIL   That's right. I sit back and I watch life. For
              instance, I can tell you that if you wanna get
              ahead in this world, you've got to be a woman,
              or a homosexual, or an immigrant. I mean, if
              you're a straight Anglo-Saxon male, forget about
              it. You're screwed. but, if you're a lesbian Sikh,
              man, the world's your oyster! That's not being a
              racist or a sexist, that's being a realist. (*beat, as
              he looks out the window*) So, what do you think,
              college boy? You wanna go over and look at the
              babes or not?

DAN   No. And I wish you'd stop doing that.

PHIL   Doing what?

DAN   Calling me college boy. I'm forty-two years old.
              I didn't even finish college.

PHIL   So, you still went.

DAN   For one year.

PHIL   Yeah, well that's one more than me. So, what do
              you think? You wanna close down for a while
              and go over?

DAN   Naw.

PHIL   You don't want to?

DAN   I don't want to.

PHIL   They got Miss Nude Venezuela over there this
              week. Huh? Get a look at some South American
              tweeters for a change.

DAN   Why? Are they any different?

PHIL   Well, that's what we're goin' over to find out.
              We'll turn it into a little fact-finding tour. Who
              knows, maybe we can get a grant.

DAN   No, thanks.

PHIL	You sure?
DAN	Yeah.
PHIL	Okay. It's just that we're not gonna get much trade through here today. Goddamn snow.
DAN	What does Darlene think of you going over there all the time?
PHIL	What? I don't go over there a lot.
DAN	Sure you do. You're over there three, four times a week.
PHIL	I am not.
DAN	You are too.
PHIL	A quick beer after work. I'm there fifteen minutes. Half an hour tops.
DAN	(*scoffing*) Fifteen minutes.
PHIL	Yes, fifteen minutes. And I only do it to wind down. I mean, I'm in here all day sellin', talkin' about this car, that car, financing, trade-ins, blue books, sticker prices. I'm doin' all this shit, and then when we're both done...I never leave until you leave, right?
DAN	Right.
PHIL	And then when we're both done I go across the street, I stuff a fiver into a G-string and bingo, I'm wound down.
DAN	And Darlene doesn't mind?
PHIL	Darlene. What, am I supposed to live my life according to her likes and dislikes?
DAN	Well, she is your wife.

PHIL	Uh-huh, well, not exactly there, Danny boy. (*stuffing another stick of gum in his mouth*)
DAN	What's that supposed to mean?
PHIL	Nothin'. She just...she left.
DAN	Darlene? She left you?
PHIL	Yeah.
DAN	Go on.
PHIL	I'm serious.
DAN	Get out.
PHIL	She did.
DAN	When did this happen?
PHIL	Couple of nights ago.
DAN	Get out.
PHIL	It's the truth.
DAN	Darlene?
PHIL	Yeah.
DAN	And you didn't tell me?
PHIL	What's to tell? She left. So what?
DAN	So what? She's your wife for godssake.
PHIL	Ahhh.
DAN	Jesus, Phil. I...I don't know what to say. I'm sorry.
PHIL	Oh, don't be sorry. It wasn't right to begin with. I shoulda seen that.

DAN	Well, listen, maybe she'll come back.
PHIL	No.
DAN	Maybe you can work things out.
PHIL	Uh-uh.
DAN	Sure. These things work themselves out sometimes.
PHIL	Dan, she's not coming back, all right? And even if she was, which she won't be, I wouldn't take her back.
DAN	Oh. It's that bad, is it?
PHIL	I'm afraid so.
DAN	Well, where'd she go? Do you know?
PHIL	Oh, yeah, I know all right. She moved in with Turk Schumacher.
DAN	The Dodge dealer?
PHIL	Hm-hmm.
DAN	Oh, no. God, Phil, I'm sorry.
PHIL	A goddamn Dodge dealer.
DAN	Jesus.
PHIL	Hey, go figure women, huh?
DAN	And you didn't even know they were...
PHIL	Had no idea. Not a clue. I shoulda known though. About a month ago she comes home with this Dodge Omni. A shitcan, right? Nothing on it. Says she bought it for herself. So, I says, what'd ya do that for? I coulda put you in a loaded Tempo at cost plus the dealer

discount. She says she doesn't want me buying
her stuff. She wants to be independent.
Independent. She's never paid for a thing her
whole life. That's when I shoulda caught on.

DAN   She bought an Omni? You didn't tell me.

PHIL   Hey, it's not something I wanna spread around,
               okay?

DAN   Right.

PHIL   So, that's it. Finito. Two years down the drain.
               (*taking out comb and combing his hair*) What a
               pair though, huh? Her and Shumacher? I'll tell
               you Dan, they deserve each other. I've never liked
               that guy. Well, you know what he's like. Big
               shot, right? Vain, self-centred, always strutting
               around like some goddamned rooster. I mean, big
               deal, so he's only thirty years old and he owns a
               major dealership. Big freakin' deal, huh? Punk.

               *PHIL moves to his desk and throws his
               gum away then goes to get another
               donut.*

DAN   Before she met you, wasn't she living
               with...uh...oh, who was it?

PHIL   Harry Farmer.

DAN   Harry Farmer, Yeah. The Chev-Olds dealer,
               right?

PHIL   Right.

DAN   And before that?

PHIL   Paul Janetti.

DAN   Lincoln Mercury.

PHIL   Right.

DAN	Yeah. (*beat*) Well, on the positive side, at least she's stickin' with the North American makes. (*smirking, then laughing a little*)
PHIL	Oh, that makes me feel a whole lot better, Torelli. Thank you.
DAN	Aw, come on, Phil. I mean, you said yourself it wasn't right to begin with. For one thing she was too young.
PHIL	(*moving down, donut in hand*) What d'ya mean too young?
DAN	Well, I mean, these May-December marriages don't work out a lot of the time.
PHIL	What May-December? She's twenty-six.
DAN	And you're forty-five.
PHIL	Well, that's not May-December.
DAN	Sure it is.
PHIL	It is not. It's like June-October maybe. September even. May-December.
DAN	Well, she's still young.
PHIL	Hey, I like em' young. And if you can get 'em young, why not take em'?
DAN	Well, it didn't work out, did it?
PHIL	Maybe not, but I had a twenty-six year old in my bed for two years. When was the last time you had a twenty-six year old? Hell, when was the last time you had anybody?
DAN	Look, I'm only saying maybe you should look for someone a little older next time.

PHIL	Hey, I'll bet you wouldn't mind dipping your ladle into the fountain of youth once in a while.
DAN	No. Not under thirty.
PHIL	No?
DAN	No way. I like a woman with an advanced set of emotions and values, and that only comes with time.
PHIL	(*skeptical*) Emotions and values, huh?
DAN	Right. You, on the other hand, like a woman with an advanced set of anything else.
PHIL	And the more advanced the better. Man, I'll tell ya though, I am getting nothing but grief from women these days. First it's that tax broad and now Darlene.
DAN	Have you called that woman back yet?
PHIL	No, the hell with her. Tax audit. Like the government's gonna collapse if I don't get back to them? Come on.
DAN	Well anyway, Phil, I really am sorry about Darlene. Honest. And if there's anything I can do, you know...
PHIL	Ah, forget it. It's no problem really.
DAN	I mean, if you ever want to talk about it...
PHIL	No, really.
DAN	You're okay?
PHIL	I'm fine.
DAN	You're sure?
PHIL	Yeah.

DAN	Okay, but I'm here if, you know...
PHIL	Yeah, Yeah
	DAN returns to his newspaper. Beat, then.
DAN	A Dodge dealer, huh?
PHIL	Yeah.
DAN	Jesus. (*returning to paper*)
	Pause.
PHIL	You remember Gordie Lawrence?
DAN	Sure. He was a Dodge dealer too, wasn't he?
PHIL	That's the one. Died in that car crash?
DAN	Right. Car went off a bridge or something, didn't it?
PHIL	Right. Brand new Charger. Only had fifteen miles on it. God, what a shame.
DAN	So, what about him?
PHIL	Hmm?
DAN	Gordie Lawrence. What about him?
PHIL	Oh, nothing, nothing. I was just remembering that after he died, his wife married his partner.
DAN	That's right, she did, didn't she?
PHIL	Yeah. Boy. I wonder how long that'd been going on.
DAN	What, you think that they were...

PHIL	Are you kidding? That marriage was consummated long before Gordie and his Charger were airborne, I'll tell you that.
DAN	You think so?
PHIL	I've got a friend who works in the parts department over there.
DAN	Damn. (*going back to his paper*)
PHIL	I mean, what kind of guy would do something like that?
DAN	Hey, everybody's gotta work somewhere.
PHIL	I'm not talkin' about the parts department! I'm talkin' about Gordie's partner!
DAN	Oh. Well, it happens. You know, people mess around. Happens all the time.
PHIL	Yeah, but still...
	The phone buzzes and DAN answers it.
DAN	Doral Valley Motors. Hi Ted. Yeah, she' still coming down...Uh-huh...No, that's okay. It's a slow one here anyway.
PHIL	(*yelling*) How's everything on board the love train, Teddy?
DAN	Nothin'. Just Phil bein' a dink. Yeah...Okay...No, it's okay, really...We'll see ya. (*hanging up*)
PHIL	So, what's his problem now?
DAN	He got his car out but now he's gotta dig his wife's out.
PHIL	Doris? She drive?

DAN   Yeah, got her license last summer. You
remember that.

PHIL   No.

DAN   When you were in England. We didn't tell you
about that?

PHIL   No.

DAN   Sure we did. She got sued by that driving
instructor.

PHIL   What?

DAN   For lost wages. Come on, we didn't tell you
this?

PHIL   No.

DAN   Oh, Christ, she put the car into somebody's
family room over on King Street.

PHIL   You're kiddin' me.

DAN   No. This couple's sittin' there watching t.v. and
the next thing you know, they're staring down
the business end of a Buick Skylark.

PHIL   (*laughing*) No.

DAN   Yeah. God, the instructor was in a body cast for
two months.

PHIL   Ted's wife, Doris?

DAN   Yeah. So, the guy sues her and just before they
get to trial her lawyer calls his lawyer and tells
him what their defense is gonna be. She's gonna
say that she went off the road because the
instructor was copping a feel.

PHIL   No!

DAN	Yeah. The next day they settle out of court for like five hundred dollars.
PHIL	And was he?
DAN	What, copping a feel? Come on, Phil, you've seen Doris.
PHIL	Geez, I didn't know any of this.
DAN	I thought you knew.
PHIL	How am I gonna know unless somebody tells me?
DAN	Well, anyway, that's what happened.
PHIL	Coppin' a feel. The things some women say, huh?
DAN	(*back to paper*) Tell me about it.
PHIL	God. (*beat*) It's like Darlene. Some of the things she said.
DAN	(*not looking up*) What things?
PHIL	Well, before she left, you know? We had this fight and, I don't know, I guess I called her a couple of names, and then she said some things. I mean, just to get me back I guess, ya know?
DAN	(*looking up*) Oh, Yeah? Like what?
PHIL	Oh, crazy things. nothing that made any sense really, just...she was just ranting.
DAN	Yeah, well, hell hath no fury. (*going back to paper*)
PHIL	Yeah. (*beat*) For instance she said she got it on with you once.
DAN	(*beat*) What?

PHIL	Yeah. Do you believe that?
DAN	What do you mean got it on with me?
PHIL	She was ranting.
DAN	You mean, she...her and me?
PHIL	Yeah.
DAN	When? When did she say this happened?
PHIL	Forget it. It's crap.
DAN	I wanna know.
PHIL	It doesn't matter.
DAN	Phil.
PHIL	About a year and a half ago at the beerfest, all right?
DAN	What beerfest? At the dealer's convention?
PHIL	Yeah.
DAN	She said we did it at the beerfest?
PHIL	Well, not *at* the beerfest. She said you did it...in the parking lot. In your car.
DAN	In my...Phil, I drive a Tercel for godssake. How in the hell am I gonna get it on with a woman in a Tercel?
PHIL	Hey, that's what I told her.
DAN	You know what the leg room's like in my car.
PHIL	Dan...
DAN	Sure, I've got the reclining buckets, but still...

PHIL   Dan, I told you, I didn't believe her.

DAN   How could she say that?

PHIL   She was mad. I called her a couple of names and she got mad, that's all.

DAN   I mean, we're partners. How long we been partners?

PHIL   Twelve years.

DAN   You're damn right twelve years. And before that, how long did we work together at Jerry's?

PHIL   Nine years.

DAN   Nine years. So twenty-one years I've known you. No way I'm gonna get it on with your wife.

PHIL   I know that.

DAN   Huh?

PHIL   I know.

DAN   And in a Tercel?

PHIL   Hey, women say things sometimes.

DAN   Yeah, but really...

PHIL   It's just talk, that's all.

DAN   That's all it is, you know.

PHIL   It's talk.

DAN   That's all it is.

PHIL   You didn't think I believed her, did you?

DAN   Why wouldn't you believe her? The woman's been under more car dealers than B. F. Goodrich for godssake.

PHIL   Hey, please.

DAN   Sorry.

PHIL   I'll tell you why I wouldn't believe her. Two reasons. First of all, you're not her type. Darlene goes for the...well, you know, the stronger virile type guy. No offense intended.

DAN   No, I understand.

PHIL   I'm just stating a fact here. I mean, you're no Paul Newman, right?

DAN   I understand. Perfectly.

PHIL   And reason number two, and most importantly - trust. I trust you.

DAN   Well, I should think so.

PHIL   After twenty-one years? Of course I trust you.

DAN   All right.

PHIL   All right.

DAN   Beerfest.

PHIL   It's laughable.

DAN   It's a joke.

PHIL   God. That's why we've lasted so long, you and I, you know that? Because we've always been straight with each other. I know that if there was something going on between you and Darlene, you'd tell me about it, right up front.

DAN	Hell, if I could do it in a Tercel I'd take out an ad. (*going to get a coffee*)
PHIL	If there was anything you thought I should know about...
DAN	Anything.
PHIL	I know you'd come and tell me. Right?
DAN	Do you even have to ask? Of course I'd tell you. And I hope you'd do the same for me.
PHIL	You know I would.
DAN	All right.
PHIL	All right.
DAN	(*still making his coffee*) God.
PHIL	Women, huh? Do yourself a favour, Dan. Don't get married again.
DAN	I'll think twice, I'll tell you that.
PHIL	Of course, you were lucky your first time around. That Connie was a princess. I mean it. And cute? God, she was adorable. Huh?
DAN	You don't have to tell me.
PHIL	I guess not. No sir. How long's it been now anyway?
DAN	Almost three years.
PHIL	Three years. You still miss her, do you?
DAN	Yeah. Yeah, I guess I do.
PHIL	Yeah. For a while there after the accident I didn't think you were gonna come around at all. Man, were you depressed. I couldn't blame you though.

DAN   It was you got me through it, Phil.

PHIL   Ah.

DAN   No, I'm serious. You were there for me. Right from the start. When I called you from the hospital that night...I mean, I didn't know what to do. I was in shock, and you came right down. I haven't forgotten that.

PHIL   It was a terrible thing, Dan. A young woman like that. That's the way it is though, huh? It's always the good ones that go young. That's something Darlene won't have to worry about. She'll be test driving car dealers until she's a hundred. (*unwrapping another piece of gum and putting it in his mouth*) Oh, guess who I ran into last night?

DAN   Who?

PHIL   Bill Woodley. The guy who owns that running shoe place? What's it called?

DAN   Feet First.

PHIL   Right. Yeah, you sold him a car not too long ago, right?

DAN   Yeah. Turbo Coupe.

PHIL   Right. He mentioned that.

DAN   (*moving to his desk with coffee*) So, where'd you run into him?

PHIL   Holloway's. Yeah, I went in for a drink last night and he was in there with his wife.

DAN   Oh. So, how's the car?

PHIL   Great. Says he loves it.

DAN   Good.

PHIL   Yeah, no problem. We talked for quite a while in
              fact. He seems like a nice guy.

DAN   Yeah. Yeah, he is. I mean, I don't know him that
              well, but...

PHIL   No?

DAN   No. Well, I see him around once in a while but...

PHIL   Well, from what he told me, you've been talking
              to him quite a bit lately. Says he offered you a
              franchise.

DAN   What?

PHIL   A franchise. A store.

DAN   Oh. Oh, hell, that was nothing.

PHIL   No?

DAN   No. I mean, we talked about it but not seriously
              or anything.

PHIL   You sure?

DAN   Positive. It was over drinks. You know how you
              talk about things over drinks.

PHIL   Well, he seems to think you're serious. He said
              he wouldn't have said anything to me but he
              thought I knew already. He thought you told me.

DAN   There's nothing to tell. We threw the idea around
              and that was it. It was just...you know...It. was
              nothing.

PHIL   It was just talk?

DAN   Yeah.

PHIL   You mean, you're not considering it?

DAN	No. Well, I'm not ruling the idea out entirely. I mean, athletic wear is a booming business right now.
PHIL	Then you are considering it.
DAN	No. I'm just not discounting it, that's all.
PHIL	Oh.
DAN	I mean, it's always nice to have options, right?
PHIL	Sure. But, what the hell do you know about selling shoes?
DAN	Athletic wear. It's not just shoes, it's jogging suits, it's sweat shirts, it's a whole line of active outerwear.
PHIL	Active outerwear?
DAN	Yeah.
PHIL	Active outerwear? You sound like you already bought this thing.
DAN	No, I haven't already bought it.
PHIL	But you are thinking about it.
DAN	Yes, I am.
PHIL	You wanna be a shoe salesman?
DAN	It's not just shoes...
PHIL	Why in the hell would someone wanna do that instead of this?
DAN	I didn't say I did.
PHIL	You wanna sell goddamn shoes?
DAN	I just wanna have options.

PHIL   What the hell for?

DAN   What do you mean, what the hell for? I've been in this business for twenty-one years, Phil. Look at this. (*holding up the paper*) Jerry Henderson. Thirty-five years selling cars, and what does he get? Survived by his wife Mary. That's a hell of an epitaph isn't it? Well, not for me.

PHIL   And selling shoes is gonna change that, is it?

DAN   It might change people's perception of me, yes. You know what the public thinks of car salesmen, Phil? Huh? They think we're crooks. Fast-talking sleaze balls with bad taste in clothes. That's us. Idiots who make fools of themselves in television commercials. (*doing a mock TV commercial*) You want deals, friends?! We got deals! Nobody walks away from a Doral deal! Remember, we're in the valley so don't dilly dally! No wonder my son thinks I'm an asshole.

PHIL   What does he know? He's gay.

DAN   He's not gay! Jesus! The thing is, Phil, I don't wanna wind up like Jerry. Hustling cars at fifty-five. I don't want that. There's gotta be something else.

PHIL   Like what? Hustling active outerwear? Come on, Dan, face it, you're a car salesman. You're a lifer here.

DAN   No, I'm not.

PHIL   You are.

DAN   No. No. You maybe, but not me.

PHIL   So, what does that mean? You're buying the franchise?

DAN   I didn't say that.

PHIL	Well, are you buying it or not?
DAN	I don't even know why I bother talking to you about it. You're not gonna understand. (*moving to get his coat*)
PHIL	Not when you talk about something stupid like bein' a goddamn shoe salesman. What the hell is that?
DAN	You see? That's exactly what I mean. Exactly. (*going to the door*)
PHIL	Where you goin'?
DAN	I'm goin' out for lunch.
PHIL	Lunch? It's barely eleven.
DAN	So what?
PHIL	Is that what time shoe salesmen take lunch? Eleven?
DAN	I feel like lunch now, all right?
PHIL	What's the problem?
DAN	Nothing.
PHIL	What is it?
DAN	Nothing. Just forget about it.
PHIL	You're pissed off because I think the sneaker thing is a dumb idea.
DAN	(*moving down again*) You don't know anything about it, Phil. You don't know one thing about it, and yet you think it's stupid. How can you do that? How can you judge something you don't know the first thing about?
PHIL	It's a gift. I guess I'm blessed.

DAN	Yes, Phil, I guess you are.
	DAN moves to the door again.
PHIL	So, where you goin'?
DAN	Next door to Ling's.
PHIL	What, for Chinese?
DAN	Yes, for Chinese.
PHIL	Take out?
DAN	No, I'm gonna eat it in.
PHIL	You never eat in.
DAN	Well, today I am.
PHIL	You always bring it back here. We always get take out together and bring it back here.
DAN	Well, not today. I feel like doing something different today, okay? Jesus. You know what we're doin' here Phil? Huh? We're rotting. That's what we're doing. We're decaying.
PHIL	Now what's the problem?
DAN	Our lives. Our day-to-day stinking lives. That's the problem. Here. (*moving to pick up the paper*) You know how many times a day I read this same newspaper? Huh? Four times a day. The same damned paper. And in between, I sit around waiting for some poor schmuck to come through that door so I can sell him some piece of shit that he doesn't even want to buy in the first place. And I'm supposed to feel good about that? Huh? And you. Wasting your life across the street there watching the strippers.
PHIL	Oh, come on. Fifteen minutes a day I'm in there...

DAN	(*exploding*) Bullshit, fifteen minutes! Bullshit. You go over there at six, you go home ten, eleven o'clock. What the hell kind of a life is that, Phil? Huh?
PHIL	How do you know what time I go home?
DAN	(*ignoring his question*) No wonder you can't keep a woman. No wonder they screw around on you for godssake.
PHIL	That's none of your business.
DAN	You're damn right it's my business.
PHIL	Oh? And why's that, Dan?
DAN	Because we're partners, remember? We're partners! And I'm tired of watching you mess up.
PHIL	What, mess up? I'm in here, I'm on, man, and you know it. I'm the best.
DAN	Fine. Think what you want.
PHIL	I've carried you for twelve years, you dumb son of a bitch!
DAN	(*pausing*) Right. Right you are, Phil. (*starting for the door*)
PHIL	Hey. (*trying to lighten up*) Hey, come on, Dan. I was kidding. Jesus. You don't know when I'm kiddin' anymore? Dan, you need a woman worse than I thought. You're wound up tighter than a drum. What're you gettin' so serious about?
DAN	It's about time one of us got serious.
PHIL	What the hell for? What's the point?
DAN	Everything's a joke to you, isn't it?
PHIL	Damn right.

DAN	Well, fine. You go ahead and live like that, but don't expect me to. (*moving for the door*)
PHIL	Hey? (*as DAN doesn't stop*) Dan?
DAN	(*angry*) What?!
PHIL	Are you really goin' for Chinese?
DAN	Didn't I say I was goin' for Chinese? I'm goin' for Chinese.
PHIL	How about bringing me something back? Huh? For my lunch.
DAN	(*taking a deep breath*) Like what?
PHIL	Anything. I don't care.
DAN	Well, like what? What do you want?
PHIL	I don't know. A dinner.
DAN	You want the dinner for one?
PHIL	Fine. Dinner for one. Terrific.

DAN starts to leave.

Sweet and sour pork, maybe. Get some of that too.

DAN	That doesn't come with the dinner for one.
PHIL	Well, then get it separate.
DAN	Plus the dinner for one?
PHIL	Yeah.

DAN starts to move again.

No. No, forget the dinner for one. Get the sweet and sour pork and a couple of egg rolls.

DAN	No dinner for one?
PHIL	Right. Just the pork and the egg rolls.

DAN starts to move again.

Some soup too I guess.

DAN stops.

Actually just the soup and the egg rolls. It's too early for the pork.

DAN	So, you don't want the pork.
PHIL	Right. Just the uh...No, I'll tell you what. Get me the dinner for one. The hell with it.
DAN	Just the dinner for one?
PHIL	Right.
DAN	No soup, no egg rolls.
PHIL	Right.
DAN	No pork.
PHIL	Right. You want me to write it down?
DAN	No.
PHIL	You seem to be having trouble remembering it.
DAN	Dinner for one. I've got it.
PHIL	You want some money?
DAN	No.
PHIL	Here. Let me give you some money. It's my turn to buy anyway. Here you go. (*handing DAN some money*) Dinner for one. Maybe some soup too, I don't know.

DAN   Do you want the goddamn soup?

PHIL   It doesn't matter. Surprise me.

> *DAN exits and PHIL moves to the door, calling after him.*

Get me some Chiclets too! (*to himself*) Goddamn snow.

> *Lights down. End Act One, Scene One.*

Act One, Scene Two

*About an hour later. As the scene
opens, PHIL is seated at his desk. He is
talking on the phone. A wastebasket
sits on top of Dan's desk. There are
crumpled up pieces of note paper on
DAN's desk and on the floor around it.
PHIL is tearing pieces of paper from a
note pad on his desk. He crumples the
paper up and attempts to toss them into
the wastebasket as he talks.*

PHIL   I know, Ted (*throwing a piece of paper toward
the wastebasket, then ripping another piece from
the note pad*)...Yeah...Well, if you've got a bad
back you shouldn't be shovelling snow in the
first place, should you? You know what else you
don't do with a bad back?...Sex...well, because of
all that movin' around. You'll throw something
out...Oh, well, if you don't move around much
then fine, go right to it...No, it's slow. Yeah.
They're packin' em' in across the street though.
Damn right...Miss Nude Venezuela. Forty-eight
inch maracas from Caracas...Tell you what. What
say you come in about two and we'll go over and
have a look, huh?...No, we'll be there fifteen
minutes.

DAN enters with two paper bags.

Doris'll never know...Yeah, well, think about it...Okay. We'll see ya. (*hanging up*) Well, it's about time. What were you doin' over there? Makin' time with Ling's daughter?

DAN I wasn't gone long. I was gone an hour.

> *DAN sets the bags on PHIL's desk then hangs up his coat.*

PHIL Oh. Seemed longer. So, how was lunch?

DAN I didn't eat.

PHIL You didn't eat?

DAN I had a coffee.

PHIL I thought you went over to eat.

DAN Well, when I got over there I didn't feel like it.

PHIL So, you had a coffee.

DAN I had a coffee.

PHIL And you didn't eat.

DAN I didn't feel like it.

PHIL (*beat*) So, you sat there for an hour and had a coffee.

DAN Yes, Phil.

PHIL And no food.

DAN Yes! And then I ordered a dinner for one to go, and I brought it back here, and now I'm going to eat it, all right?! (*picking up one of the bags and moving to his desk*)

PHIL So what'd you get me? You get the sweet and sour pork?

DAN   No. You said you didn't want the pork. You said
             it was too early for the pork.

PHIL   Yeah, but that was an hour ago.

DAN   So, what, you want the pork now?

PHIL   No, forget it.

DAN   You want me to go back and get the pork?

PHIL   No.

DAN   I'll go back and get the pork.

PHIL   No, this is fine. What is it?

DAN   It's the dinner.

PHIL   (*looking in the bag*) No soup?

DAN   You said you didn't want the goddamn soup.

PHIL   I said maybe the soup. I said surprise me.

DAN   All right. Surprise! You didn't get the fucking
             soup!

PHIL   (*pausing as he gets his food out*) So, was she
             there?

DAN   Who? (*moving to clear the pieces of paper off his
             desk and putting the wastebasket on the floor*)

PHIL   Ling's daughter.

DAN   I don't know. I didn't notice.

PHIL   Didn't notice?

DAN   I didn't notice.

PHIL   How can you not notice the girl? She's gorgeous.

DAN	She's eighteen years old for godssake.
PHIL	Yeah, I suppose you're right. God, if I was only five years younger. (*eating now and looking into the empty bag*) Where's the Chiclets?
DAN	Oh, shit, I forgot them.
PHIL	You forgot the Chiclets?
DAN	I forgot them. I'm sorry.
PHIL	Jesus. No Chiclets, no pork...
DAN	Do you want the pork? I'll go back and get the goddamned pork. (*moving to his coat*)
PHIL	Forget about it.
DAN	No, I'm gonna get the pork.
PHIL	Dan, forget the pork. I don't care about it.
DAN	Well, then stop talking about it.
PHIL	Fine.
DAN	Christ! (*moving to his desk*)
PHIL	It's the Chiclets I really wanted. I'll tell you something though. If that girl's eighteen, I'm Lee Iaccoca. She's gotta be nineteen, twenty at least, huh?
DAN	Who?
PHIL	Ling's daughter. She's nineteen, twenty at least.
DAN	She's still too young.(*sitting down to his lunch*)
PHIL	Maybe. First girl I ever had was nineteen, and to me that was an older woman. I was sixteen. I've told you this story, haven't I?

DAN	Seven or eight times.
PHIL	Ah. (*taking a bite, then, after a beat*) Just turned sixteen in fact. My folks used to rent a place up on Morgan's Lake every summer and we'd go there for a week or two. Best summers I ever had were spent up there. Anyway, this girl, her folks rented the cabin next to ours one year and I guess it was just dumb luck that I was the only teenage male for ten miles.
DAN	Phil, I've heard this.
PHIL	Yeah, but not in detail.
DAN	Yes, in great detail.
PHIL	I told you about the rapids?
DAN	Yes.
PHIL	The short shorts?
DAN	Yes.
PHIL	*The Girl From Ipanema*?
DAN	(*beat*) No, that's new.
PHIL	All right, so, this girl and I get pretty friendly and one day we take a walk up to where the lake narrows into almost like these rapids, you know?
DAN	What, you're gonna start from the beginning?
PHIL	What?
DAN	I've heard all this.
PHIL	I thought you wanted to hear about *The Girl from Ipanema*.
DAN	Yeah.

PHIL   Well, it's coming up.

DAN   You can't skip right to it??

PHIL   No, I can't skip right to it.

DAN   Why not?

PHIL   Because it needs a lead in. Christ! You know nothing about storytelling at all, do you?

DAN   I just thought you could skip right to it.

PHIL   Well, I can't skip right to it, all right? Geez. So, we go to these rapids. Water's about three, four feet deep maybe and in the middle of this narrow section, there's this —

DAN   Big flat rock.

PHIL   Right. Poking up just above the surface. Just stickin' up there like some sort of serving tray. And so this girl, Lesley, wades into the water and climbs up on this rock to sunbathe. She's wearin' this bikini top —

DAN   And the short shorts.

PHIL   And she is hot. So, she's up on this rock and I don't know what to do, I mean, I'm sixteen, right? I'm on the shore there kickin' at the dirt wonderin' should I go over and sunbathe with her or what?

DAN   And then she calls to you and waves you over.

PHIL   But I say, no, maybe I'll just head back, right? Dad wants me to clean some fish or somethin' I say. God, we can be stupid at sixteen. But, then she waves me over again. So, I kick off my shoes and wade on over to her. And when I get up on the rock I find that there's room up there for maybe a person and a half, and while we're lying there, our legs are rubbing together —

DAN   And your shoulders are touching.

PHIL   And every once in a while the water sprays over us and out of the corner of my eye I can see her wet stomach, and her chest rising and falling as she breathes. And under her breath, so you could hardly hear her, she's singing *The Girl From Ipanema'* (*singing*) Tall and tan and young and...Well, God, every nerve in my body had gone to condition red, you know? So, after about five minutes of this, she reaches down and takes my hand...

DAN   Okay, I know the rest. You went the whole nine yards.

PHIL   Right there on that rock. And the whole time she's singing *The Girl From Ipanema* (*singing*) God. You wanna know the truth, Dan, and this is something I've never told you..

DAN   All right, you're not gonna get graphic are you, because I'm eating here.

PHIL   I was just gonna say that I haven't had it as good since. I even thought I was in love with her. Sixteen huh? You get these crazy ideas. But, she left the next day and I never saw her again. Maybe that's why I have a thing for these younger women, huh? Maybe I'm still looking for that nineteen-year-old named Lesley. Ah, anyway, you're right. I should forget women altogether. I'm gettin' too old for this shit. You know what I hate about being older?

DAN   What?

PHIL   You won't laugh, right?

DAN   No. What?

PHIL   Love handles.

                        DAN laughs.

                I'm serious. You can't avoid them. It's like you
                turn forty, you look down and there they are. Oh,
                sure, it's all right for someone like you, but
                when you're married to a younger woman, you're
                thinkin' that she could find someone younger
                who...you know?

DAN   Doesn't have them?

PHIL   Yeah, something like that.

DAN   Like Turk Schumacher.

PHIL   Goddamn punk. (*beat*) So, what do you say?
                How about a beer?

DAN   No.

PHIL   Sure, let's break out a couple. We're not gonna
                get anybody else in here today. Might as well
                enjoy ourselves, right?

                        *PHIL moves to where the coffee is,
                        opens a small ice box, and pulls out
                        two bottles of beer.*

DAN   Well, okay. Maybe one.

PHIL   Sure. One beer. What the hell? So, how come
                you've never told me about your first time?

DAN   What?

PHIL   Your first time. You've never told me about it.

DAN   Ah, it was nothing.

PHIL   How old were you?

DAN   Uh...I was sixteen too.

PHIL Yeah, that seems to be the popular age. Of course these days, Jesus, who knows? (*bringing DAN's beer to him*) So, why haven't you ever told me about it? What's the big secret?

DAN It's no big secret. I just told you. It was nothing.

PHIL So who was she? Someone at school.

DAN No.

PHIL What then? A summer love like mine?

DAN No.

PHIL Well, who was she?

DAN She was just a person I knew.

PHIL An older woman?

DAN Yeah.

PHIL Yeah, they're the best. I mean, you get a girl nineteen, twenty, with a little experience in the trenches and they can make it a whole lot easier for you. There's none of this fumbling around in unfamiliar territory, ya know? They can put the car in the garage the first time out. So, how old was she?

DAN Thirty-four.

PHIL (*almost choking on his beer*) Thirty four?!

DAN Uh-huh.

PHIL Three four?

DAN Yeah.

PHIL You?!

DAN Yeah. Whaddya mean, me?

PHIL   Jesus, Dan. You're supposed to work up to a
            thirty-four year old? You don't *start* with them.
            You got nowhere to go if you do that. Who the
            hell was she?

DAN   It was just someone I knew.

PHIL   What, one of your school teachers?

DAN   No.

PHIL   A neighbour? The lonely housewife type?

DAN   Come on.

PHIL   Well, who was it then?

DAN   Nobody.

PHIL   Come on, whaddya being so mysterious about?

DAN   I'm not. It's just personal.

PHIL   What, too personal to tell even me?

DAN   Yes.

PHIL   Oh. Well, all right.

DAN   Oh, so what, are you gonna pout now?

PHIL   Hey, it's none of my business. You as much as
            said that. So, let's drop it.

DAN   It was my stepmother, all right?! Satisfied?!

PHIL   (*beat*) Your...you mean, your Dad's —

DAN   My Dad's wife, right.

PHIL   No. You boffed your mother?

DAN   Stepmother.

PHIL   God, I had to go to Morgan's Lake to get mine.
You just had to go into the kitchen.

DAN   Phil!

PHIL   Wow. I think you're the only guy I know did
that. Gus Brown over at Hilltop Towing put it to
his sister-in-law once but, Christ, a mother.

DAN   Stepmother.

PHIL   Isn't that incest or something?

DAN   No!

PHIL   Well, you can sure see it from there, by God.
Jesus. So, what happened? Were you pissed off at
your Dad or something?

DAN   No.

PHIL   Well, I'll bet he was sure pissed off at you.

DAN   He never found out. He died not long after it
happened.

PHIL   Probably what killed him. God, Dan. I mean, a
guy like you? I would've never thought.

DAN   All right, Phil, just leave it alone, will ya? Just
let it rest.

PHIL   Hey, it's forgotten. Like I never heard it. She
seduce you or what?

DAN   Yes.

PHIL   Wanna talk about it?

DAN   No.

PHIL   I do.

DAN	Look, she seduced me, okay. Her and my Dad, I don't know, they just weren't getting along and one weekend my Dad went away with some friends, and that's when it happened. That's it. It only happened once, and I moved out right after. End of story.
PHIL	Boy, I'll bet you felt like a real dirtbag, huh?
DAN	Can we just not talk about it?
PHIL	Hey, fine. We'll change the subject.
DAN	Thank you.
PHIL	Geez, your mother.
DAN	Are we changing the subject?
PHIL	We're changing it. Absolutely. (*beat, taking a sip of beer*) So, why does your son think you're an asshole?

DAN flashes PHIL a dirty look.

	Well, do you wanna change the subject or not? You said your son thinks you're an asshole. So, why?
DAN	He doesn't think that. He just...I guess he doesn't think much of his old man being a car salesman, that's all.
PHIL	Why? What'd he say?
DAN	Nothing. That's just it. He never says anything about my job. It's almost like he's embarrassed, I don't know. And there's the other thing too, you know, with Connie. I mean, he was more Connie's boy and I guess he hasn't gotten over it yet.
PHIL	He still blames you for it, doesn't he?

DAN	Maybe. I don't know.
PHIL	Well, hell, it wasn't your fault.
DAN	No, but it was supposed to be me picking him up from his hockey game, not her. If I hadn't gotten tied up here that night, she wouldn't even have been driving.
PHIL	Well, that doesn't make it your fault for Chrissake. A drunk runs a stop sign, how does that make it. your fault?
DAN	Well, kids see things differently. The black and white of it is, if she isn't driving that night, she's still alive.
PHIL	Well, I hope you don't see it that way. Huh?
DAN	No.
PHIL	I should hope not. Man. I mean, if you want to look at it that way, then maybe you should blame me.
DAN	Oh, come on...
PHIL	No, I'm serious. I mean, if I didn't get called away like I did, then you wouldn't have had to stay here that night, right?
DAN	Phil...
PHIL	But, it was Vicki. You know how Vicki was. Everything was an emergency with her. At least once a week she'd call here with some problem that I had to rush home for.
DAN	I know.
PHIL	Well?
DAN	I know, I know.

PHIL   All right then. God. These things like what
         happened to Connie, they're just the result of like
         a hundred other things happening that no one can
         see coming. Vicki calls me, says the basement's
         flooded, I gotta leave, you gotta stay, Connie
         goes to pick up the kid, a guy, I don't know
         what, has a fight with his wife maybe, gets
         drunk, runs a stop sign. I mean, if Connie leaves
         the house two minutes earlier, she's still here. If
         the guy leavin' the bar fumbles with the lock on
         his car for ten seconds for Chrissake, then she's
         still here.

DAN   I know Phil.

PHIL   Well, there's no way he should blame you. If he
         wants to blame someone, tell him he can blame
         me, all right?

DAN   Nobody's gonna blame you, Phil.

PHIL   Well, just tell him anyway. Better he blames me
         than his old man. Families have got to stick
         together. That's something I believe in very
         strongly.

DAN   Since when?

PHIL   What, since when? Since always.

DAN   You don't even have a family.

PHIL   So, what? I can't believe in them because I don't
         have one? I don't have an electric chair either but
         I still think they're a good idea. Boy. I mean, it's
         not like I didn't want to have a family. Not with
         Darlene but with Vicki maybe. We talked about
         it a lot, Vicki and me.

DAN   So, why didn't you have one?

PHIL   What?

DAN   A family. Why didn't you have one?

PHIL	Because.
DAN	Because why?
PHIL	Because none of your business.
DAN	None of my business?
PHIL	None of your business.
DAN	After I told you I slept with my stepmother, now I get 'none-of-my-business'?
PHIL	This is private.
DAN	And sleeping with my stepmother isn't??
PHIL	Hey, you didn't have to tell me about that. I didn't even wanna know about it.
DAN	You hounded my ass about it!
PHIL	I inquired.
DAN	The hell you did. Now, come on. Why didn't you have any kids?
PHIL	(*beat*) All right, but you don't tell another living soul. This stays right here. You don't even tell Ted. All right?
DAN	Fine.
PHIL	All right. (*beat*) The...uh...the truth is, I didn't have the right stuff.
DAN	You what?
PHIL	You know. I didn't have it. My body betrayed me.
DAN	You mean, you can't perform?
PHIL	Hell, yes! Of course I can.

DAN	Well, what do you mean?
PHIL	I mean I'm...I'm sterile.
DAN	Oh.
PHIL	It doesn't mean I can't do it. I mean, I can do it. I'm not like that.
DAN	Impotent.
PHIL	Impotent, right. Hell, yes, I can do it. I just don't have enough of the, you know...
DAN	Sperm. You don't have a high sperm count.
PHIL	I don't have enough to raise a goddamned onion. But I can make it. There's no problem there.
DAN	I believe you.
PHIL	I mean, I can give you references. As long as your arm.
DAN	As long as my arm?
PHIL	The reference list.
DAN	Oh.
PHIL	Damn right. And you can start with Darlene. She'll vouch for me. We were at it five or six times a week. Hell, I'm surprised she had the strength to get up and leave me.
DAN	Why didn't you ever tell me this?
	GAIL PIERCE enters. She is dressed for the weather and carries a big bag over her shoulder.

PHIL	Well, it's not like I'm gonna walk in one morning and say 'Hey, guess who's got a low sperm count?' (*seeing GAIL*) Oh, good afternoon, ma'am.
GAIL	(*smiling*) Gentlemen.
PHIL	How are ya today? (*going to her*)
GAIL	Oh, fine.
PHIL	Good. Quite a day out there, isn't it?
GAIL	Yes, it certainly is.
PHIL	(*turning on the salesman charm*) Of course, I've always liked the snow myself. I don't know what it is. Maybe it's because a fresh blanket of snow seems to give the city that Norman Rockwell kind of look. (*holding out his hand*) Phil Moss. Welcome to Doral Valley Motors.
GAIL	(*shaking his hand*) How do you do?
PHIL	And this is my partner, Dan.
GAIL	Hello.
DAN	Hi.
PHIL	So, what brings you out on a day like this?
GAIL	Well...
PHIL	No, wait a minute. And I call myself a car salesman. You're probably here because it *is* a day like this, right? Sure. What are you driving?
GAIL	Uh, it's a...
PHIL	I'll bet it's not front-wheel drive. Am I right?
GAIL	Well, as a matter of fact, it's not.

PHIL	Uh-huh. Now that's not entirely bad. Don't get me wrong. But, in weather like this, if I don't have front-wheel drive I don't pull out of my driveway. How old's the car?
GAIL	Four years.
PHIL	Well, it should have a good trade-in value, so you're gonna save yourself some money there. Now, are we looking at a smaller vehicle or are you gonna have that family in tow?
GAIL	Well, I don't have a family, so...
PHIL	Well, you're gonna save yourself some money again. The smaller vehicle, as a rule is gonna run you less, plus it's more fuel-efficient, and I don't have to tell you about the price of gas these days. Boy, you've been here all of what, a minute and a half, and we've saved you five, six thousand dollars already. Now, don't worry. This isn't a sales pitch. We don't make sales pitches here at Doral. We let the customer do the dealing. Can I get you a coffee?
GAIL	No, thank you.
PHIL	Donut?
GAIL	No.
PHIL	Well, just look around then, and if you see anything you like on the lot out there, give us a shout.
GAIL	Well, actually —
PHIL	Oh, wait, wait, wait. You know what? I just had a thought. Dan, that Isuzu that came in last week, that's front-wheel drive, right?
DAN	Sure is.

PHIL	(*to GAIL*) You know, maybe we can save you some time as well as money. How would you like to get yourself into a front-wheel drive this very afternoon?
GAIL	Well, no, I don't —
PHIL	Now, I'm gonna be honest with you, this has been a slow day for us and I really would like to sell something even if we don't make much on it. I just wanna move some of the inventory out. I mean, it doesn't look good to have the same cars sitting on the lot week after week. Makes the competition think we're standing still, but you didn't hear that from me. Dan, what do you think? Can we knock maybe five hundred off the price for...I'm sorry I didn't get your name.
GAIL	Gail. But —
PHIL	Gail. (*to DAN*) Can we do that for Gail?
DAN	On what, the Isuzu?
PHIL	Yeah.
GAIL	(*to DAN*) No.
DAN	Gee, I don't know, Phil. That's really pushing it. She's already down close to the invoice price as it is.
PHIL	Yeah. Yeah, I guess it is. (*to GAIL*) Sorry, Gail. I mean, we do have to make something on the deal. I'm not gonna deny that we're in this business to make a profit. But, maybe we can find something else for you. Something not quite as flashy maybe but hey, maybe you're into that no-nonsense-straight-ahead kind of vehicle. I mean, I wouldn't think so to look at you, you look kind of adventurous, but what do I know? Dan's always telling me what a bad judge of character I am so maybe I'm wrong. Dan, what do you think? Gail here? Adventurous or not?

DAN	Definitely adventurous.
PHIL	You think so?
DAN	Definitely.
PHIL	(*to GAIL*) So I'm right for once. So maybe the Isuzu is for you...
GAIL	Mr. Moss —
PHIL	But like I say, we can only go so far before we...now, wait a minute. Wait, I'll tell you what. You know, what I'm gonna do? Now, you're gonna think this is crazy, but just go with it for a second. (*taking out a chequebook*) I mean, ordinarily I wouldn't even consider doing this but what the heck? The Lord hates a coward, right? Gail, I'm gonna write you a check (*to DAN*) You'd better stop me, Dan. I'm gonna do something nuts. Here's a cheque for three thousand dollars, Gail, right now. Three thousand dollars for your old car. Sight unseen. What do you think of that?
GAIL	Well —
PHIL	(*to GAIL*) This way, we can get you into the Isuzu at the sticker price and we'll take the chance on moving your trade-in at a higher resale.
GAIL	But, I —
PHIL	(*to DAN*) Now, Dan, I know what you're going to say. Three thousand dollars, sight unseen? It's lunacy. But, I've already promised the lady, so if it doesn't fly, it comes outta my pocket. Every penny. (*to GAIL*) Now, I don't want you to feel pressured, Gail. I've told you we don't like to make sales pitches here at Doral. We want you to make the decision. If you don't want the Isuzu just say so.
GAIL	Well —

PHIL	In fact, I'll tell you what. I wanna give you some time to think it over, so, I'm gonna go into the boardroom there and write out the cheque for you, and maybe my partner here can take you out on the lot and brush off the car so you can have a look see. Dan, could you do that?
DAN	Sure.
PHIL	Thanks. (*to GAIL*) And don't forget. There's no obligation here, Gail. If you don't like the vehicle then you don't even have to come back inside. You can just climb into your...is it rear-wheel drive?
GAIL	Yes.
PHIL	Just climb into that rear-wheel drive of yours and swish on out of here. All right? I'll be right in here. Take all the time you need.

PHIL exits to the boardroom.

GAIL	Mr. Moss?
DAN	(*moving to GAIL*) We haven't been formally introduced. It's Dan Torelli.
GAIL	Gail Pierce.
DAN	You know, I think you'll like the Isuzu, Ms Pierce.
GAIL	Uh, actually, I didn't come here to buy a car.
DAN	You didn't?
GAIL	No, you see, I'm from Revenue Canada. (*handing him a card*)
DAN	(*beat*) I'm sorry?
GAIL	Revenue Canada? The tax people.

DAN	Oh, the tax people, right. Right. I...I've heard a lot about you. Well, not *you* in particular, but you people. As a group I've heard about you. So ...what brings you by?
GAIL	Well, I'm here to see Mr. Moss, but he didn't give me a chance to tell him. He's quite the salesman, isn't he?
DAN	Oh, yes, ma'am. Phil there could sell arms to the Swiss. Not that he'd do that you understand. He just...(*calling*) Phil, could you come out here please?

PHIL enters with a cheque in his hand.

PHIL	Oh, you're still here. Good. Gail, I forgot to get your last name for the cheque here. See that? (*showing it to GAIL*) How does that look? Pay to the order of Gail...?
GAIL	Pierce.
PHIL	Pierce. Three thousand dollars. (*writing her name on the cheque*)
DAN	Phil?
PHIL	It's not very often three thousand dollars falls into your lap this easily, huh? And even when it does, the vultures at the tax department wind up takin' half of it anyway, right?
DAN	Phil?
PHIL	Boy, they get you comin' and goin' don't they? And they wonder why people cheat.
DAN	Phil, Ms Pierce, isn't here to buy a car.
PHIL	Well, of course she isn't. Nobody comes in to buy a car. They come in to look. (*to GAIL*) But, I think that once you see this vehicle, Gail...

DAN	Ms Pierce is from Revenue Canada.
PHIL	Oh, good. Good. Did I mention the rebate on the Isuzu? That's gonna bring this check up to almost four thousand...
GAIL	So, we finally meet face to face, Mr. Moss. After two months of talking to your answering machine I was beginning to worry that this day might never come.
PHIL	(*playing dumb*) I'm sorry. Answering machine?
GAIL	Yes. At first we sent you notices, but after getting no response to those we began a vigorous phone campaign.
PHIL	You've been trying to get hold of me, have you?
GAIL	Just about every day.
PHIL	And you sent notices you say? I didn't get any notices.
GAIL	Well, we sent them. Six of them in fact.
PHIL	To my home?
GAIL	We thought that would be the best place.
PHIL	Well, there's the problem right there. I...I don't live there anymore.
GAIL	You don't?
PHIL	No. You see well, the truth of the matter is, I'm going through a marriage break-up right now and I've moved in with my partner Dan over here. Isn't that right, Dan? This is Ms Pierce from the tax department.
DAN	I know.
GAIL	Mr. Moss is living with you, is he?

DAN	Well...for the moment, yes, but I believe he's moving back to his own place this afternoon, isn't that what you said, Phil?
PHIL	That's right. (*to GAIL*) You see, my wife has...well, the sad truth is she's moved in with another man, so I'm moving back to my own place again. I don't expect it'll be easy. I mean, the apartment holds a lot of memories for me, but, I've been a burden to Dan here for too long now. Do you believe that, Dan? Ms Pierce has been calling me and sending me notices and Darlene didn't even have the decency to tell me. My God.
GAIL	Mr. Moss, you are being audited.
PHIL	I'm sorry. I'm what?
GAIL	Your past three tax returns are being audited. A few discrepancies have come to our attention and we'd like to clear them up.
PHIL	Audited.
GAIL	That's right.
PHIL	Me. You're auditing me?
GAIL	I'm afraid so.
PHIL	I see. (*to GAIL*) Well, this comes as quite a shock. What kind of discrepancies are we talking about here?
GAIL	Well, we can go into detail when we do the actual audit.
PHIL	Uh-huh. Well, all right. Fine. I've got nothing to hide. When do you want to get together? Next week is bad for me, but maybe the week after that we —
GAIL	Today.

PHIL	I beg your pardon?
GAIL	Today. Now. Can we use your boardroom?
PHIL	Oh, today is bad. Very bad. Saturday's our busiest day, isn't that right, Dan?
DAN	Very busy.
GAIL	But a moment ago you said it was slow.
PHIL	Well, I was trying to sell you a car then.
GAIL	I see. And what are you trying to do to me now?
PHIL	Nothing.
GAIL	Good. Now, we're going to need any slips or receipts you may have from the last three years. I'm sure you've kept them?
PHIL	Uh, well...
GAIL	I mean, you are supposed to save them for seven years, you know that.
PHIL	Sure. Sure, I've got them, but they're...they're at home.
GAIL	Yes, but you don't live far from here.
PHIL	Yes I do. Yes. Quite far in fact. Miles, I think.
GAIL	Chester Street, right?
PHIL	Yes.
GAIL	Yes, I just came from there. I stopped at your apartment first, thinking I might find you there. It's about a five minute drive.
PHIL	Five minutes? Gee, I hope you weren't breaking any laws.

GAIL   No. Now, why don't you go ahead and get whatever you have for me and I'll get set up in here. (*moving to the boardroom*) Hopefully, we can clear this up in one afternoon.

PHIL   Listen, are you sure you want to do this today?

GAIL   Yes, quite sure.

PHIL   But, it's Saturday.

GAIL   So?

PHIL   So, you're a civil servant; you people don't work on Saturdays.

GAIL   This civil servant does. I've been trying to close this case for two months, and now that I'm this close, I'm not going to let you slip away. Hurry back.

GAIL exits to the boardroom.

PHIL   Well, this is great. This is just great. I am screwed right here and now.

DAN   Did you cheat?

PHIL   No, I didn't cheat. I was creative maybe, but I didn't cheat. Man, I can't believe this. First my wife buys a Dodge, and now a civil servant goes to work on a Saturday. The fuckin' world must be comin' to an end.

End Act One.

Act Two

It is a few hours later. As the scene opens DAN sits at his desk reading the newspaper. The door to the boardroom opens and PHIL enters followed by GAIL. PHIL is looking a little disheveled now: loose tie, jacket off, sleeves rolled up. He moves to pour himself a coffee and GAIL follows, tax forms in hand.

GAIL   All right, now what about this one?

PHIL   Look, can you give me a break while I get a coffee here?

GAIL   Please, we're almost done. Now, you claimed your wife as a dependent a year before you married her.

PHIL   So?

GAIL   So you can't do that.

PHIL   Why not?

GAIL   Because you weren't married.

PHIL   But, we lived together for part of that year.

GAIL	That's not the same as being married to her.
PHIL	Lady, you got that right. It was okay when we were just living together. Getting married is what screwed things up. (*to DAN*) You watch, Dan. Whaddya wanna bet Darlene tries to get half of everything I own? (*to GAIL*) Which by the way, isn't very much.
GAIL	Mr. Moss, you cannot claim your wife for that year.
PHIL	Fine. Scratch her off then, all right? In fact, you can scratch her off for the time I could claim her too. Let's just forget her altogether. Boy, the last time I had it put to me this good I was naked and being kissed. (*moving to DAN*)
GAIL	Our only goal, Mr. Moss, is to see that everyone who is supposed to pay, does, in fact, pay.
PHIL	Oh, well don't worry, I pay all right. Every time I turn around I'm paying. I pay sales tax, luxury tax, school tax, road tax, property tax, surtax, excise tax, goods and services tax, If it's a goddamned tax, I'm payin' it, all right? I only wish you people could think up more taxes, you know, because I never get tired of payin' 'em. Isn't that right, Dan? How many times have I said to you, 'Goddamn it, I've got some extra cash in my pocket, I'm gonna get those tax people on the phone'. (*to GAIL*) No, don't you worry, Ms Pierce. I'm paying.
GAIL	Fine. Now, about this political contribution.
PHIL	What about it?
GAIL	Well, you've stated here that you made a contribution of five hundred dollars to a political party.
PHIL	So?

GAIL	So, you didn't enclose a receipt to verify that contribution.
PHIL	Sure I did.
GAIL	No, I'm afraid you didn't.
PHIL	I did. I put it in with all the other receipts.
GAIL	Well, I'm afraid we didn't receive it.
PHIL	Oh, what, so that's my fault? You people lose my receipt and I'm supposed to answer for it. What the hell kind of system is that?
GAIL	We also did not receive receipts for a three hundred dollar contribution to a Save the Bison organisation, and a two hundred and fifty dollar donation to the United Nations.
PHIL	Well, they were in there too, with all the rest. Jesus. What else did you lose?
GAIL	(*remaining calm*) We didn't lose them, Mr. Moss.
PHIL	No? Well, somebody sure as hell did.
GAIL	They weren't enclosed with your return.
PHIL	Well, I say they were. (*to DAN*) Do you believe this, Danny? You see what we're up against in this country? Incompetence.
GAIL	I assure you, my department is quite competent.
PHIL	Yeah, well I think different. (*to DAN*) You see what I told you about me and women? First Darlene and now her. (*to GAIL*) You know, you're the only woman who's ever given me this much hassle without I didn't marry her first. (*to DAN*) Not that I'd want to. I don't think even Westinghouse could defrost this one.

GAIL

Hey! I'm not invisible Mr. Moss. If you've got something to say you can say it to me, all right? And please make it fast because I'm running out of patience.

PHIL

You're running out of...(*to DAN*) You hear that? I'm being treated like a goddamned felon over here, and she's running out of patience. Let me tell you something honey. I'm being audited here for one reason and one reason only. Because you and your department fucked up. Pardon my French. And you know something else? It's an insult to have my integrity questioned like this. Now, why don't you just pack up your little files and get out, okay? I've got work to do.

> *PHIL moves to the file cabinet near his desk and opens it.*

GAIL

Well, I've got work to do too, Mr. Moss. And despite what you might think, we are a very efficient group. We do not lose —

PHIL

(*cutting her off and ignoring her*) Dan, did you run a credit check on that Miller woman? The Topaz?

DAN

Uh. Yeah. Yeah, it's all on her sheet in there.

> *PHIL turns and looks through the file.*

GAIL

(*after a beat*) We do not lose receipts which are properly enclosed —

PHIL

(*to DAN, cutting her off again*) So, is she okay, or what? Did she clear?

DAN

Yeah. Yeah, she cleared.

PHIL

Good.

> *PHIL pulls out a file and begins to read .*

GAIL   (*after a beat*) You know, I don't like dragging my tail out here in this kind of weather to try and nail down deadbeats like you. In fact, it's the part of my job I hate the most. Do you think you're the only foul-mouthed windbag who's tried to cheat on his taxes? Well, you're not. Not by a long shot. I get one of you guys kicked my way every single day, and you're all the same. It's never your fault, it's our fault. We lost your receipts or we didn't add it up right or we missed this deduction and that deduction. Well, I have had it. I've listened to so much of your crap this afternoon I feel like I'm about to choke on it. So, you can ignore me, Mr. Moss, but I am not going away. And I am not your honey. You got that? And I didn't fuck up, you fucked up! And unless you can justify it, your ass is mine!

PHIL   (*beat, then still somewhat defiant*) Whaddya gettin' so pissed off about? I'll find the receipts, all right?

GAIL   You go right ahead.

PHIL   Fine.

GAIL   Fine.

                                PHIL exits to the boardroom. GAIL looks at DAN who goes back to reading his paper.

GAIL   I'm not a bad person you know.

DAN   I didn't say a thing.

GAIL   I mean we're not the government bounty hunters that everyone thinks we are. We only look into the returns that our computer says might be dirty.

DAN   Like Phil's?

GAIL Alarms went off when his was checked. We thought there was a fire on the floor.

DAN Well, I hope you'll excuse his attitude. He really is going through a break-up right now.

GAIL Hey, a lot of us are. That's no excuse for being a horse's ass.

DAN No. no, I suppose it's not.

GAIL I'm sorry. I shouldn't have mentioned that. I should keep my personal and professional lives separate.

DAN Right. Good idea.

GAIL Of course, that is why I'm working on a Saturday. They say you should keep busy when you're going through a traumatic experience, right? So, here I am. Well, not that it's that traumatic. I mean, after all, he's only a man. It's not like losing a family pet or anything. I'm sorry. I'm sure you don't want to hear this.

DAN No, that's okay. It's...uh...you know I think I'll get a coffee. Would you like a coffee? (*moving to get coffee*)

GAIL No thanks.

DAN No?

GAIL No. (*beat*) Actually, I haven't talked to *anyone* about it yet. He's been gone two weeks and I haven't even told my mother yet. I'm not sure why exactly. I guess I'm ashamed.

DAN Well, it's nothing to be ashamed of. Marriages fail all the time.

GAIL	Oh, not mine. My marriage was perfect. In fact, my life was perfect. I'd never failed at anything. Straight A student all through school. Married the best looking boy in college. Over achiever at work. I was running my department by the time I was twenty-five. Model wife for fourteen years. At least that's what I thought. Ah, I don't even want to talk about it.
DAN	(*moving down with his coffee*) Hey, I don't blame you. It's a tough time. (*looking at snow*) Boy, it sure is coming down out there.
GAIL	And then all of a sudden he says he wants some space. He says he's not sure he wants to be a couple anymore. Says he needs to be on his own so he can discover himself again. Find his individuality.
DAN	Men.
GAIL	Personally, I think he's found another woman. You know, someone a little younger, a little prettier maybe. God, that scares the hell out of me. I mean, to be used up and tossed away at thirty-six? Her name's probably Debbie. It's the Debbies you've gotta watch out for. The Debbies and the Shelleys. You married?
DAN	Widowed.
GAIL	Oh, that I could take. At least then I'd know why he's gone. And where he's sleeping at night.
	DARLENE MOSS enters dressed in a winter coat and boots.
DARLENE	Hi, Dan.
DAN	(*surprised to see her*) Darlene. Uh, hi.
DARLENE	Hi.

DAN	What are you doing here? I mean, it's okay that you're here, it's just that...well, Phil's not here. I mean, he's here, but he's in a meeting.
DARLENE	That's okay. I just came by to drop off my key to the apartment.
GAIL	Well, I'd better get back in there. Excuse me. (*exiting to boardroom*)
DAN	Well, nice to see you.
DARLENE	Yeah, you too.
DAN	Quite a day out there, isn't it?
DARLENE	Yeah.
DAN	Yeah. (*awkward pause*) So, I hear you've got a new car dealer. Car! A new car.
DARLENE	Yeah.
DAN	How's it working?
DARLENE	Better than the old one.
DAN	Good. Good.
DARLENE	Rides a lot better.
DAN	Uh-huh.
DARLENE	Doesn't run out of gas as quick either.
DAN	Better mileage, huh?
DARLENE	Yeah.
DAN	Yeah. A Dodge is it?
DARLENE	Uh-huh.
DAN	Good. Good car, Dodge.

DARLENE   Yeah. And I really like the smell of a new car too, you know?

DAN   Hey, who doesn't?

DARLENE   Yeah. There's something. about it that...oh, I don't know. It does something to me.

DAN   Really?

DARLENE   They should bottle that smell and sell it as men's cologne.

DAN   Yeah. That's an idea.

DARLENE   So, I guess you've heard, huh?

DAN   Heard? Oh, you mean about you and Phil? Yeah. Just this morning.

DARLENE   Oh, well. Que sera sera, right?

DAN   Yeah.

DARLENE   (*moving down*) So, what did he tell you?

DAN   Oh, not much. Just that you left a couple of days ago, and...well, that you, you know, moved in with Turk Schumacher.

DARLENE   Oh.

DAN   Is that true?

DARLENE   Yeah.

DAN   Uh-huh.

DARLENE   So, how have you been?

DAN   Fine. Fine.

DARLENE   I haven't seen you.

DAN   Well...

DARLENE   You used to come around once in a while. What
                 happened?

DAN   Oh, you know, I get busy. I've got...you know,
                 I'm workin' on the house every spare minute I
                 get.

DARLENE   You're renovating?

DAN   No. Just, you know, vacuuming, dusting.

DARLENE   Uh-huh. Are you and Phil not getting along?

DAN   Who, me and Phil? Naw. You know me and
                 Phil. We're like brothers.

DARLENE   So, how come you don't come around?

DAN   I told you.

DARLENE   Vacuuming and dusting.

DAN   Right.

DARLENE   Is it me?

DAN   What? No.

DARLENE   You sure?

DAN   Positive. You? Why would it be you?

DARLENE   Well, if it is, you don't have to worry about that
                 anymore.

DAN   Well, it's not.

DARLENE   You can come around anytime you like now. I
                 won't be there.

DAN   Darlene, it's not you. Okay?

DARLENE	Okay.

Awkward pause.

DAN	So Turk Schumacher, huh?
DARLENE	Yeah.
DAN	Hmm-hmm.
DARLENE	You don't approve?
DAN	Hey, it's not my place to approve or disapprove. It's just that —
DARLENE	Just that what?
DAN	Well, I mean, Turk Schumacher. I just think you can do better, you know? I mean, a city this size, almost a million people, there's gotta be a thousand car dealers out there.
DARLENE	Turk's okay.
DAN	Okay?
DARLENE	Well, at least he shows me some attention. At least he spends time with me. Phil...Phil's never around. He's always over there. (*pointing to the strip joint across the street*) And even when he was around, he never talked to me. He said we didn't have enough in common to talk to each other. You know, because of our ages. Well, just because I'm young, doesn't mean I'm stupid, does it?
DAN	Not necessarily.
DARLENE	That's right. I can talk about lots of things that he likes to talk about. I know a lot about cars.
DAN	Well, you should. I mean, you know, married to Phil and all.

DARLENE   And I know more than just cars too. I mean, what's his problem? If you can't talk to a person, why would you marry them in the first place?

DAN   I don't know, Darlene.

DARLENE   I thought he loved me.

DAN   Well, you know, in Phil's own way, I think he does.

DARLENE   He's never told me. Not once.

DAN   What do you mean? You mean never?

DARLENE   Never.

DAN   You mean, you married him and you didn't talk about whether or not you loved each other?

DARLENE   Well, I just assumed. I mean, he asked me to marry him. I just figured that was like saying I love you. I guess it wasn't.

DAN   And what about Turk? Has he told you he loves you?

DARLENE   Yeah.

DAN   When?

DARLENE   What do you mean, when? Lots of times.

DAN   Like when? Like...like when you're just sitting around?

DARLENE   Yeah.

DAN   Before sex?

DARLENE   Yeah.

DAN   During?

DARLENE	Dan.
DAN	Well?
DARLENE	Yes, during.
DAN	What about after? Does he tell you he loves you after?
DARLENE	I don't know. What difference does it make? I do know that with Phil it wasn't before, during or after.
DAN	Maybe he just can't say the words.
DARLENE	Well, I'm sorry, but I've got to hear them. Even if it's only once. And besides, Phil and I weren't having sex...that much anyway.
DAN	You...what do you mean?
DARLENE	We didn't have sex that much. I mean at first we did, sure, but then it got down to about once or twice a month.
DAN	Once or twice? You and Phil?
DARLENE	What's the matter? Does that surprise you?
DAN	Well, I mean, to listen to Phil talk, it sounded like...well, you know.
DARLENE	Well it's not. At least not with me. I mean, I'll bet I could tell you the day of the week and where it happened every time we did it the last two months.
DAN	No, no. Please, Darlene, I'll take your word for it.
DARLENE	Maybe he's getting it somewhere else.
DAN	Phil? No.

DARLENE	Are you sure?
DAN	Positive. God, if anybody would know, I would, right?
DARLENE	Oh, that's a laugh.
DAN	What?
DARLENE	You think you know everything about Phil?
DAN	More than most.
DARLENE	Well, you didn't know he was seeing me when he was married to that Vicki.
DAN	(*beat*) He what?
DARLENE	You see? You didn't know that.
DAN	Phil was cheating on Vicki? With you?
DARLENE	For the whole last year of their marriage. He'd leave here early sometimes, come over to my place for a couple of hours and then go home. Sometimes I'd even call him so you'd think it was his wife asking him to come home. Anyway, you're probably right. He's probably not seeing anyone now. Of course, it might be best for him if he was. I don't know how Phil's gonna make out on his own. He's not the loner type, you known. He's always gotta have somebody around. How long is he gonna be in this meeting anyway?
DAN	Uh...well, it might be a while yet. He's being audited.
DARLENE	Audited? You mean like for tax stuff?
DAN	Yeah.
DARLENE	Oh-oh. They must've found out about the deposit business, huh?

DAN The what?

DARLENE The deposit thing. You know.

DAN No, what deposit thing?

DARLENE Come on. He said you guys do it all the time.

DAN Do what?

DARLENE Come on, Dan. You sell a car for say, ten thousand dollars, and you get the buyer to leave a five hundred dollar deposit. Then you write the sale up at ninety-five hundred and you pocket the deposit, So, is that why he's being audited?

DAN Uh...I don't know. I think they just found something wrong with his return that's all.

DARLENE Well, I hope they don't hit him up for too much. He's only got a couple of thousand in the bank as it is. So, what about you? You seeing anybody?

DAN No.

DARLENE Nobody at all?

DAN Afraid not.

DARLENE Oh, that's too bad. Everybody should have somebody, don't you think?

DAN Well, I just haven't found the right one yet I guess.

DARLENE Yeah. Of course. Sometimes I think somebody who's only halfway right is better than nobody at all. It's like sex that's only half good. It's never really bad, Is it? (*looking at new car poster on the wall*) What is that smell anyway, Dan? In a new car? Why does it smell like that?

DAN I don't know, Darlene. Could be the leather. Could be anything.

DARLENE   Could it be Armour-all?

DAN   Yeah, I suppose.

DARLENE   I'll have to get some.

                PHIL enters from the boardroom.

PHIL   I'm telling you, Dan, this — (*stopping when he sees DARLENE*)

DARLENE   Hi, Phil.

PHIL   What are you doin' here?

DARLENE   Well, what kind of greeting is that? Don't you say hi or anything?

PHIL   Hi. What are you doing here?

DARLENE   I came to give you my key to the apartment.

DAN   (*standing*) Maybe I'll take a little walk.

PHIL   No, stay. You heard her. She only came to give me a key.

DARLENE   Well, I thought maybe we could talk too.

PHIL   Talk about what?

DARLENE   Well, you know? Just talk. Say good-bye?

DAN   Yeah, I'll take a walk.

PHIL   No, stay. (*to DARLENE*).What do you mean say good-bye? What, do you wanna kiss me off twice?

DAN   Phil...

PHIL   No, I mean it. (*to DARLENE*) What's to talk about? You left. And now you wanna say good-bye? You're supposed to do that *before* you leave.

DARLENE   I don't want us to be mad at each other.

PHIL   Mad? Why would I be mad? Because you were seeing a Dodge dealer behind my back and now you're living with him? Hell, I'm surprised I don't feel a song coming on.

DARLENE   It's not just me that's to blame here, Phil.

PHIL   No, no, of course not.

DARLENE   There were two of us in the marriage.

PHIL   Yeah, well only one of us moved in with the Dodge dealer.

DARLENE   Oh, come on, Phil. Can't we be civil about this?

PHIL   No, Darlene, we can't be civil. Not when there's a Dodge dealer involved.

DARLENE   All right, fine. Be a stubborn bastard then. (*starting to root through her purse*)

PHIL   Hey, I gotta be me.

DARLENE   Oh, right. We don't want Phil Moss changing for anybody, now do we? Here. Here's the key. (*handing it to him*) And I guess I'll be filing for divorce but I don't know when. Or you can if you want. It doesn't matter. I mean, you've got me for adultery, so if that's what you want to do then go ahead.

        DAN gets up and moves toward the washroom.

DAN   Excuse me.

PHIL   Where are you goin'?

DAN   I'm gonna use the john.

PHIL	What, right now?
DAN	Yeah, right now.
PHIL	You can't wait?
DAN	I don't want to wait. Why should I wait?
PHIL	Well, we're talkin' here.
DAN	*You're* talkin'. I'm not talkin'. You're talkin'.
PHIL	Seems like a funny time to use the john.
DAN	Is there a non-funny time to use the john?
PHIL	Well, I mean, right when we start talkin'?
DAN	Go figure! Now, go ahead. Talk. Talk. (*exiting to the washroom*)
DARLENE	Well, Phil?
PHIL	Well, what?
DARLENE	Do you want to file for divorce or not?
PHIL	(*beat*) Look, I've got a hundred other things to look after right now. I can't be...
DARLENE	All right, then I'll file. Is that what you want? (*beat*) Well?
PHIL	Do whatever you like.
DARLENE	Fine then. And I'm going to have to come over sometime and get the rest of my things. You know, dishes and pictures and things. So, maybe I'll do that next week.
PHIL	Right.
DARLENE	Right. Well, that's it then.

PHIL	I guess so.
DARLENE	You've got the key.
PHIL	Yep.
DARLENE	So I guess I'll see you then.
PHIL	Take care of yourself.
DARLENE	(*moving to the door, then turning back*) Did you ever really love me, Phil? I mean, you know, really love me?
PHIL	I married you didn't I?
DARLENE	But, did you love me?
PHIL	What do you wanna know that for?
DARLENE	Just say it. Yes, or no?
PHIL	Why?
DARLENE	Because. Now, did you or didn't you? I mean, even in the beginning when we were good together. When I seemed to make you happy. Did you love me even then?
PHIL	Well, it doesn't matter a helluva lot now, does it?
DARLENE	It might. (*beat*) Did you, Phil?
PHIL	(*beat*) I, uh...look, I've got somebody waiting here. I've gotta get back.
DARLENE	Phil...
PHIL	Really. I gotta go.
DARLENE	Right. Well, I guess it doesn't matter a helluva lot then. (*turning to leave*)
PHIL	Call me.

DARLENE	(*stopping*) What?
PHIL	Call me. You know, if you...when you wanna come over and get those other things. Give me a call.
DARLENE	Good-bye, Phil.
	DARLENE exits. DAN enters from the washroom.
PHIL	Women, huh? Jesus. (*beat*) Did you ever wish you were a kid again, Danny? When the only thing you had to worry about was whether or not your mother was cooking cauliflower that night? Or whether or not you could impress your old man by standing up on a pair of skates. Crazy, isn't it? The only relationship that's ever worked out for me is this one. Hell, you and me, we've lasted longer than both my marriages put together. Figure that one out. (*looking out the window*) Still packin' em' in over there. Good God, she must be something else to have them coming out in weather like this. Course, they've got the roast beef special over there too. That doesn't hurt.
DAN	Phil?
PHIL	What?
DAN	I know this isn't the best time, but there's something we've got to talk about.
PHIL	What, you too? Why all of a sudden today does everybody want to talk to me? Huh? I'll tell you something, Dan, I'm learning something here. When people want to talk to you it's bad news. It's better nobody wants anything to do with you.
DAN	Phil, I've been thinking about that other thing.
PHIL	What other thing?

DAN   With Bill Woodley.

PHIL   What, the shoes?

DAN   Yeah. I think I'm gonna buy in. I should've told you this morning, but I wasn't a hundred percent sure, and besides, it wasn't a good time. I mean, things were kind of heated, you know?

PHIL   Oh, well this is a much better time. Thank you.

DAN   Anyway, now I'm sure.

PHIL   Come on.

DAN   I am.

PHIL   But...what, you're just gonna leave?

DAN   Well, soon. I mean, I'm gonna need some capital for the franchise buy, so I'd like to sell out here as fast as I can.

PHIL   (*smiling as if he's caught on to the joke*) You son of a bitch.

DAN   What?

PHIL   You son of a bitch. I know what this is. Huh? You think I'm partners with someone for twelve years and don't know when I'm being conned?

DAN   Conned? Phil —

PHIL   You're gettin' me back because I made fun of you, right? Because of the shoe thing?

DAN   No, it's not...

PHIL   Dammit you almost had me too, you bastard.

DAN   Phil, I mean it.

PHIL   Yeah, right.

DAN	It's not a joke. I'm gonna call Bill today.
PHIL	Hey, go ahead. Call him right now.
DAN	Phil, I'm serious
PHIL	(*picking up his phone*) Here, use my phone if you want. Come on.
DAN	Phil, I'm getting out.
PHIL	(*angry*) The hell you are! (*slamming down the phone*) Goddamn it! I am not gonna let you throw away what we've built up here.
DAN	And what's that? What have we built up, Phil? What?
PHIL	You know what. This place was dying when we took it over. We put it back on it's feet.
DAN	Just barely.
PHIL	It's lasted twelve years, hasn't it? That's pretty damn good if you ask me. Jesus, Dan, we've made a name for ourselves in this business.
DAN	Right. Like Jerry did.
PHIL	Forget about Jerry! Jerry was good, man, but not like us. He couldn't touch us. And I've got some ideas about how we can get even bigger. Yeah, I've been thinkin' maybe we buy out Ling's. Then we level the place and open up some lot space where we can put in maybe fifty, sixty more units. We'll double our inventory.
DAN	Phil, we can't even move what we've got out there now.
PHIL	That's because we look like a small operation. You see that? It's cosmetics.

DAN   The way I see it, Phil, there are two things we
             can do. You can buy me out if you want, or...

PHIL   Oh, don't start with that.

DAN   Phil, listen to me, all right?! This isn't easy for
             me either. Now, you can buy me out if you
             want, or I can sell it to a third party. I haven't
             approached him yet, but I think Ted might be
             interested. But, that's only if you approve. I
             mean, I won't sell to anybody who doesn't get
             your okay.

PHIL   I should've seen this coming, you know?

DAN   Phil...

PHIL   From the very first day you started in this
             business, you thought being a car salesman was
             beneath you. All the guys, we all knew it. But,
             you hung in there. I don't know why, but you
             did.

DAN   The steady money, that's why.

PHIL   No, it was more than that. I know you too well
             to think that you stayed just for the money. It
             was Connie, wasn't it?

DAN   Connie?

PHIL   She was the one who liked the steady money,
             right?

DAN   No. She didn't care.

PHIL   Well, she got you the job.

DAN   Who told you that?

PHIL   Jerry. Connie's Dad and Jerry were old buddies,
             right? And when Connie got pregnant she got her
             Dad to get you the job, and then she made you
             drop out of college.

DAN

She didn't make me drop out. I didn't have any choice. We were gonna get married, we had no place to live. We needed money fast.

PHIL

Hey, you don't have to tell me. I think you did the right thing. I just wonder why you stayed at it so long if you're so goddamned embarrassed by it.

DAN

And I suppose you're not.

PHIL

No! I love this business. I mean, say what you will. Tell me it's not important what we do, tell me the public thinks we're a bunch of sleaze balls, but, goddamn it, I love selling cars. It's one of the few things in this life that I've turned out to be good at. I mean, when I come in here every morning, I know I'm gonna be tested. Damn right. Every sale is different. Every customer. They're all gonna come up with ten different reasons why they shouldn't buy a car from me and I've gotta come up with ten other reasons why they *have* to. Why they absolutely *must*. And by the time I'm through with them, if I've done my job, they're gonna be thinking, 'If I don't buy this car from this guy, my life is going to be pig shit.' And then there's that second when you close the deal. That instant when you realise you've won. Call me crazy, Dan, but that excites me.

DAN

Well, it doesn't excite me, Phil. It never has. You know, in my whole life I haven't done one thing that I'm proud of. Not one thing.

PHIL

What are you talkin' about? What about this place? The way we turned things around here?

DAN

Phil, you don't understand. This isn't what I had planned for my life. Somewhere along the way I got lost, and now I want to try and get back on track.

PHIL	By selling shoes?! You're gonna be proud of that?
DAN	It's not just shoes, goddamn it!
PHIL	You can't even say it, can you? You're gonna be a goddamn shoe salesman and you can't even bring yourself to say it. Jesus, that's pathetic.

> *DAN turns away to his desk and PHIL follows.*

PHIL	Come on, Dan. You can't leave and you know it. We're partners. Partners don't let each other down.
DAN	Oh, don't they?
PHIL	Absolutely not.
DAN	Phil tell me about the deposits.
PHIL	What deposits? What's that?
DAN	The deposits. You been pocketing deposits, which means you've been stealing money from me.
PHIL	What? What the hell are you talking about?
DAN	We're in this business fifty-fifty, right? All the sales we make we split fifty-fifty. It doesn't matter whether you sell twenty cars and I sell one or I sell forty cars and you sell none. We split the profits fifty-fifty.
PHIL	Sure we do.
DAN	So, how long have you been pocketing the deposits? How much have you taken over the years? How much of my money?
PHIL	You're talkin' crazy.

DAN   Phil, stop lying to me! I know all about it!

PHIL   (*beat*) Darlene, right? She told you.

DAN   It doesn't matter who told me.

PHIL   Boy, she doesn't miss a trick, does she?

DAN   Is that how you paid for that trip to England last year? With my money?

PHIL   Hey, we asked you to come along, didn't we?

DAN   If I'd known I was paying for it I would have!

PHIL   It wasn't even that much. A couple of grand. Three or four maybe.

DAN   You screwed me around, Phil? Is that what partners do to each other? They screw them around?

PHIL   I don't know, Danny, you tell me. You're the expert.

DAN   Tell you what?

PHIL   Come on, tell me. Tell me what partners do to each other. Huh? What do they do?

DAN   You stole money from me, Phil.

PHIL   I'll tell you what they do, college boy. At that dealer's convention? The beerfest?

DAN   Phil...

PHIL   No, you listen! I remember. I was talking to John Ritchie. You know John. Does the leasing for Schumacher's outfit. So, I'm talkin' to John, and I look at my watch and it's like one thirty, so I figured it was about time I gathered up Darlene and called it a night. That was when John's wife tells me that she just saw Darlene leave with you. Well, of course I figure that Darlene's had too much to drink like she always does, and you're taking her outside to get some air. So, I go outside to see what I can do. Your car was in the far corner of the lot. Way the hell out there. And when I got outside Darlene had you up against the car. I didn't go any further than the front door but I could see you out there. Boy, she was giving you the goin' over real good. And then the two of you got into your car. That's when I went back inside. I talked to John and his wife for another fifteen, twenty minutes maybe. I have no idea what we talked about but I do know that was about the longest twenty minutes of my life. Then Darlene came back, and soon after that, you came in. That was you out there wasn't it? That was your car? (*as DAN doesn't answer*) Or maybe my eyes are going like the rest of my body, huh? Huh?! You wanna know when I started skimming deposits, Danny? The very next day.

DAN   (*beat*) If you cared about her, Phil, you should have showed her, and if you didn't then you shouldn't have married her.

PHIL   Oh, I see, so it's my fault.

DAN   No, it's not your fault, but you you're just like my old man was. The people who are closest to you, you drive them away. First Vicki and then Darlene...

PHIL   And now you.

DAN   No, not me. You were right, Phil. My heart has never been in this business. I started in this business because I needed the money and that's it. But with the kids out on their own now, it's my turn. I've gotta do something else. Anything else. Phil...honest to God, I'm so sorry about what happened.

PHIL   (*beat*) Ah, forget it.

DAN	No, I can't.
PHIL	(*brushing it off*) Hey. I mean, it's not like you were trying to steal her away from me, right? Were you?
DAN	No.
PHIL	Well all right then. Forget about it.
DAN	Phil, she was your wife, and I made love to her.
PHIL	You had sex with her. In a car. A Tercel for godssake.
DAN	There you go again. Talking about the woman as if she was nothing. Why do you do that?
PHIL	Because if I told you how I really felt, I might want to break your neck. And besides, I think maybe you owed me that.
DAN	What do you mean, owed you?
PHIL	(*beat*) The, uh...the night Connie was killed, the phone call I got from Vicki?...It wasn't Vicki..
DAN	Phil, never mind. I don't wanna talk about this, all right? That's over with. It's done.
PHIL	But, Dan, this is —
DAN	You know what I'm gonna do? Huh? I'm gonna take the afternoon off. Is that okay with you? (*clearing his desk*)
PHIL	Dan, wait...
DAN	In fact, maybe you should do the same. Take the afternoon off and I'll see you at the funeral tomorrow.
PHIL	Dan, please.

DAN

(*laughing a bit*) You know what the most unbelievable thing of this whole day is? The fact that you tried to convince that woman that you contributed to a Save the Bison Fund. What the hell is that, Bison Fund. That's right up there with the spider. Jesus. I'll see you tomorrow, Phil. (*starting to move*)

PHIL

You're making a big mistake, Dan. I mean, goddamn it, we're two of the best salesmen in the business you and me.

DAN

We're fair.

PHIL

Fair?

DAN

At best, we're fair.

PHIL

Fair. Do you think we would've been around this long if we were only fair? Do you think Jerry would've loaned us the money to get started if he thought we were only fair? Hell, no!

DAN

Jerry didn't loan us the money because of our salesmanship.

PHIL

You're damn right he did.

DAN

He loaned us the money because I caught him turning back odometers one night. He was afraid that I'd turn him in if he didn't loan us the money. That, plus the fact that we knew about his flings with his secretaries. He didn't want that to get back to his wife.

PHIL

What, you threatened him with that?

DAN

I mentioned it to him.

PHIL

But, Jerry was a friend.

DAN	You don't understand what I'm saying here, do you? The last twelve years, you and me...it's all been a lie. We've been living a lie. Our salesmanship, our partnership...I don't know, maybe even the friendship. It's just a bunch of lies. We can't even trust each other anymore. Damn it, Phil, after twenty-one years...I don't even know if I like you. (*looking at PHIL who remains silent*) I'm sorry. I'm going home. (*going to get his coat*) Why don't you do the same, huh? As soon as she finishes with the audit, why don't you go home?
PHIL	She's already finished.
DAN	She's done?
PHIL	Yeah.
DAN	Well, what happened? Are they making you pay or what?
PHIL	I owe a little bit. Nothing I can't handle.
DAN	Now, is that the truth or are you jerking me here?
PHIL	It's the truth. Couple of thousand. I sell one car - I'm caught-up.
DAN	Well, why don't you go home then, huh?
PHIL	No, I...I'd better hang around for a while.
DAN	Why? What's the point?
PHIL	Somebody might come in. Who knows?
DAN	Nobody's gonna come in now. It's getting worse out there by the minute.
PHIL	Well, I'll stay just in case.
DAN	Phil, come on.

PHIL	I wanna stay, all right?! I've got a business to run here.
DAN	All right. So, I'll see you tomorrow then? The funeral?
PHIL	Yeah.
DAN	Good. (*starting for the door*)
PHIL	You're wrong about the friendship, Danny.

DAN stops.

I mean, I know we're an odd couple — a guy who barely made it out of high school and a college boy over here. But no, the friendship, that's real. From my end at least. I mean, I only have but one friend in this world and, like it or not, you're it. (*almost angry now*) So, don't tell me it was a lie, because it wasn't. And you can take the other job, that's fine, and we won't be partners anymore, that's fine too. But, don't tell me I wasn't your friend for twenty-one years, you son of a bitch, because I was! I may have screwed up a couple of times and let you down, I don't know, but I never doubted for a second...not for a second...that I was your friend and you were mine. At least leave me that much.

DAN	(*beat*) I'd like to think we were friends, Phil, I really would. But I just don't know. I'm sorry.

DAN exits. After a beat the phone rings and PHIL answers it.

PHIL	Doral Valley...Yeah, Ted...no, don't worry about it. I'm, uh...I'm gonna close her up soon anyway, so...Yeah...No, nobody. Dan? He just left. Yeah. Listen, Ted, why don't you pop by anyway and we'll go across the street for a while?...Huh?...Aw, come on. We'll be fifteen minutes. A half hour tops...No, Doris'll never know. What'dya say? Fifteen minutes...No.

GAIL enters from the boardroom with her bag, putting her coat on.

No, sure I understand. No problem...Sure, we'll do it some other time.... Right. Okay, I'll see ya. (*hanging up*)

GAIL   Well, I guess that's it then. I left my card in there for you. If you have any questions you can call me at the office. (*beat*) Is there a good restaurant nearby? I haven't eaten since breakfast.

PHIL   Ling's. Right next door.

GAIL   Ling's. Chinese?

PHIL   That's right. Now, if you don't mind, I was just about to lock up. (*moving to the boardroom and turning off the lights*)

GAIL   You're leaving?

PHIL   No, I thought I'd wait around for that mid-blizzard rush we usually get in here.

GAIL   But, your sign says open Saturdays until six.

PHIL   So?

GAIL   So, it's only five o'clock.

PHIL   Lady, this business is finished. I mean, my partner just called it quits and I'll be damned if I'm gonna spin my wheels here for the rest of my life? No thank you. Only a loser doesn't know when it's time to get out. (*moving to the boardroom to turn off the lights in there*)

GAIL   This is supposed to make me feel sorry for you, right?

PHIL	Feel sorry for me? For what? I don't need this business. Jesus, I'll be glad to get the hell out of here. I mean, I've been looking around for a while anyway. You know, talking to acquaintances who could use someone like me in their organizations. Yeah, I'll make a few phone calls Monday and that'll be it. I'll be set. Now, let's call it a day, huh?

PHIL moves to his desk and begins to clear it off.

GAIL	(*beat*) You're welcome to join me if you like.
PHIL	Join you for what?
GAIL	Next door. For Chinese food.
PHIL	What?
GAIL	I know, I know. It sounds stupid. I've just finished auditing you and I've slapped you with a fifteen thousand dollar tax bill, but...I...
PHIL	You wanna ease your conscience, right?
GAIL	No. It's just that we've been at odds all afternoon and now that it's over I thought we could be civil about it.
PHIL	There's that word again. Boy, you women sure like to be civil, don't you? What, does that make you feel better when you screw us around. Huh? It's okay as long as everybody stays civil?
GAIL	There is nothing wrong with being civil. My God, you're obstinate. All right, you want the truth? The truth is, I don't feel like eating alone tonight, all right? I mean, I've been eating alone for two weeks now and I just wanted to have someone sitting across the table from me. Even if it is you. So, that's the real reason I asked you. It had nothing to do with being civil at all. In fact, I couldn't promise that I would be civil. I probably wouldn't be. I just didn't want to eat alone again.

So, that's it. I'll be going now. Thank you for your time, Mr. Moss, and good-bye.

PHIL   Ms Pierce?

GAIL stops.

I didn't contribute to the Save the Bison Fund. Hell, I don't even know if there is a Save the Bison Fund.

GAIL   Why are you telling me this now?

PHIL   Hey, it's good for the soul, isn't it? Confession? (*beat*) Good-bye Ms Pierce.

> *GAIL exits. The phone buzzes and PHIL answers it.*

Doral Valley Motors...Yes, sir...Well, we were just closing...A leasing plan? Uh...no, we don't lease cars, sir, no. In fact, Doral Valley Motors is going out of business. That's right. As of today...Yes, sir. Well, thanks for calling. Listen, sir? Let me give you some advice. Don't lease. Buy...Well, what are you getting when you lease, huh? What are you getting? It's like renting a house as opposed to buying one. We're talkin' about equity here. I mean, at least when you buy a car, you've got something to show for your investment. You can sell it if you want...(*lighting a cigarette*) Depreciation? Depreciation is over-rated, sir...absolutely. Look, I'll tell you what. Why don't you slide by on Monday and we'll talk...Yeah, I know what I said. So, we stay open one more day. So what? Besides, you don't want to drive out here today. Not in this weather...Yeah, she's coming down all right. But, you know, I kinda like the snow. I don't know what it is. Maybe it's because a fresh blanket of snow gives the city that Norman Rockwell kind of look.

*As lights begin to appropriate music up
under PHIL.*

Warranty? Oh, yes sir. One of the best in the
business. I'll tell you all about it on Monday.
You'll come in, we'll have a coffee, we'll talk.
We'll fix you right up.

Lights down, music up.

The End.

The Affections of May

Playwrights Canada Press
Toronto

The Affections of May was first produced by Theatre New Brunswick, Fredericton, 1990 with the following cast:

MAY	*Catherine Barroll*
BRIAN	*Steve Morgan*
QUINN	*Wayne Best*
HANK	*Ron Gabriel*

Directed by Michael Shamata.
Designed by Patrick Clark.
Lighting by Brian Pincott.
Stage manager - Martine Beland.

The Affections of May was subsequnetly produced by Centaur Theatre, Montreal, 1991 with the following cast:

MAY	*Bronwen Mantel*
BRIAN	*Phillip Pretton*
QUINN	*Daryl Shuttleworth*
HANK	*Michel Perron*

Directed by Maurice Podbrey.
Designed by James Cameron.
Lighting by Steve Schon.
Stage manager - Lynn McQueen.

The Characters

MAY HENNING   Between thirty and thirty-five years old.
                         Owns a bed and breakfast business.

QUINN   A man who does odd jobs around town.

HANK BEAVIS   Manager of the local bank.

BRIAN HENNING   May's husband.

All of the men are in their mid-thirties.

Act One, Scene One

The time is the present in October. The place is a bed and breakfast owned by May and Brian Henning. The set should look spacious and open. S.L. there is the exit to the kitchen and the backyard beyond. There is also a breakfast nook or cabinet of some sort S.L. A cassette player sits on the breakfast nook. There are three breakfast tables in the room, located D.R., D.C. and D.L. The table D.L. is set for breakfast. There is a newspaper on the table as well. U.L. is the front door to the home. Near the front door is a wooden coat stand and a window which looks out to the front of the house. U.R. is a set of stairs which leads to the upstairs rooms. S.R. there is a fireplace and an exit to a hall which leads to another part of the house where there is another guest room. Also somewhere in the room is a desk and telephone. This is an old house in a small town and should have that kind of feel to it.

As the scene opens, we hear the song "True Love" by Glenn Frey. May Henning enters from the kitchen carrying a basket of laundry. May is dressed casually, almost sloppily. She wears a sweat shirt, overalls, sneakers, and she has a kerchief on her head. She moves to the table D.C. and sets the laundry down. Then she moves to the cabinet, turns down the cassette, then goes to the stairs and calls up.

MAY   Brian? Breakfast! You'd better hurry, honey, before it gets cold!

> *MAY turns the music back up again and exits to the kitchen. BRIAN enters on the stairs, dressed casually, but nicely. He carries two suitcases and a sports jacket. He moves down the stairs and sets the suitcases near the front door,*

	almost in an effort to hide them from view. He hangs his jacket on the rack then moves left and turns the music off. MAY enters from the kitchen carrying a plate of bacon and eggs.
MAY	Well, it's about time sleepyhead. I've been down here for an hour already. (*giving him a peck on the cheek then setting the plate on the table*) Here you go.
BRIAN	(*hesitant*) Do you have to play that music so loud?
MAY	Sorry, Honey. I'm just in one of those moods this morning.
BRIAN	Again?
	BRIAN sits at the table.
MAY	Well, I'm feeling good, that's all. What's wrong with that?
BRIAN	Nothing. But, every day?
MAY	(*smiling*) Sorry, I can't help It. I guess you're stuck with it. (*exiting to the kitchen*)
	Offstage we hear a loud crash of pots and pans.
	(*off*) Shit! (*entering with a bottle of ketchup*) That damn thing. I'm gonna have to fix that cupboard one of these days. You can't go in there for ketchup or the coffee or anything without half the kitchen coming down on your head. (*sitting at the table*) I know what it is though. Under the shelf? One of the holdy thingys isn't holding right.
BRIAN	Could you pass the salt, please?
MAY	(*passing the salt*) Hm-hmm.

BRIAN   Thanks.

MAY   Sorry I was late coming to bed last night. I was looking over our money situation. I know, I know, I worry too much about money, but we're well into the off season now and I just wanted to make sure that we're gonna have enough to get us through. We should be all right though. We did pretty good for our first summer. (*getting up and moving to the desk in the living room*) I mean, it's a little less than we counted on but then we didn't count on having such lousy weather all summer either. (*picking up a ledger*) We've got, uh...sixty-eight hundred dollars. Now, we should be able to live on that for eight months shouldn't we? (*moving back to table*) Of course we have to pray that nothing unforeseen comes up. The pick-up worries me. I don't think it's got too many miles left on it. We should stick to driving the car. (*as BRIAN sits at the table again*) Oh, guess what I read this morning? You know that Mr. Quinn? That strange man who does odd jobs around town? His trailer burned down last night. Paper said it burned right to the ground. Fortunately, he wasn't hurt, but still...(*beat, then referring to breakfast*) How is it?

BRIAN   Fine.

MAY   You look nice this morning. What's the occasion?

BRIAN   (*becoming defensive*) What do you mean what's the occasion?

MAY   Well for getting dressed up.

BRIAN   I'm not dressed up.

MAY   Sure you are. You look good.

BRIAN   No, I don't.

MAY	Yes you do.
BRIAN	It's just an ordinary shirt and pants.
MAY	Well, you still look good.
BRIAN	But I'm not dressed up. You don't have to go accusing me of getting dressed up.
MAY	I wasn't accusing you. It's just that they're kind of dressy for chopping wood aren't they?
BRIAN	Chopping wood?
MAY	Our project for today. Getting some wood in.
BRIAN	Oh, right. I forgot.
MAY	Forgot? We just talked about it at supper last night.
BRIAN	I know, I know.
MAY	And with the big fuss I made going out and buying two new axes? How could you forget?
BRIAN	I wasn't thinking, that's all.
MAY	Did you think about the other thing we talked about?
BRIAN	What was that?
MAY	Oh, Brian. The Halloween party. You were going to think about a costume. It's only a month away you know. I still think you should be Little Boy Blue. I mean, it's a perfect match for my Little Bo Peep outfit. (*laughing to herself*) Oh, do you believe this? Who would've thought a year ago that you and I would be running a bed and breakfast in some godforsaken place called Grogan's Cove and sitting around talking about wood chopping and Halloween costumes? God, I love it. Even the newspaper is adorable.

MAY

(*picking up the paper*) *The Grogan's Cove Bugle.* Isn't that sweet? And these headlines. (*reading*) Scrabble Club Formed. Car Wash Jams. Family Stuck in Wax Cycle. Cove Hoopsters Announce Alumni Game. What's a hoopster?

BRIAN gets up taking his empty plate.

BRIAN

A basketball team.

MAY

Oh. There's more bacon in there if you want some.

BRIAN

No, no. That was fine.

BRIAN exits to kitchen.

MAY

(*still looking at the newspaper*) Honey, it says here that living in the country increases a person's life expectancy. (*reading*) Researchers say the clean air and slower pace could add as much as ten years to a person's life. (*putting the newspaper down, picking up the ledger and returning it to the desk*) You see that? If we'd moved out here ten years ago, we'd be ten years younger by now. (*laughing to herself then noticing suitcases*) Brian? What are those suitcases doing down here? (*going to laundry basket and folding clothes*)

BRIAN enters from kitchen.

BRIAN

What?

MAY

The suitcases. Did you bring them downstairs?

BRIAN

Uh...yeah. Yeah, I did. (*picking up his cup*)

MAY

What for?

BRIAN

Hmm?

MAY

What for? Why?

BRIAN	Oh. Well, I was just going to tell you in fact. I mean, I don't want you to think that I wasn't going to tell you.
MAY	Tell me what?
BRIAN	Well, I'm...uh...I'm leaving.
	BRIAN exits to the kitchen. MAY stares at the kitchen door for a moment. He enters with a dish cloth and starts to wipe the table cloth where he was sitting.
MAY	Where are you going?
BRIAN	I'm going back to the city. I called John Krause last night and he said I could have my job back if I wanted it. I start Monday.
MAY	I don't understand.
BRIAN	Turns out the fella they hired to take my place isn't working out so the timing really couldn't be better. It'll be at the same salary too, which I think is good of John seeing as how I left him in such a bind quitting like that.
MAY	Brian...
BRIAN	You know, John's a better man than I gave him credit for. He —
MAY	Brian, what are you talking about!?
BRIAN	(*beat*) I tried, May. I really did. I honest to God tried. But, I don't belong out here. This...this kind of life, it's not for me. I'm sorry. (*continuing to wipe the table*)
MAY	Sorry? Brian, we agreed to give it time. You said we'd stick with it for a couple of years at least. Didn't you say that?

BRIAN I can't do it. I just wasn't cut out for this country thing.

MAY This country thing? We put our life savings into this country thing! I gave up a teaching job to come here. And now you expect me...(*grabbing the washcloth from his hand and throwing it against the wall*) Will you stop that! And now you expect me to give it all up and move back to the city with you just because you changed your mind? That's not fair, Brian. I won't do it!

BRIAN picks up the dish cloth.

BRIAN I'm not asking you to move back, May. (*exiting to the kitchen*)

MAY (*a little unsure of herself*) Well, what's that supposed to mean? Brian?

BRIAN enters from kitchen.

What are you saying?

BRIAN Well, you're happy here, right? So stay.

MAY Stay? You mean I stay and you go?

BRIAN Sure. I mean, just because we're married doesn't mean we have to do *everything* together.

MAY What, not even live together? We're not going to live together, why did we bother to get married nine years ago? Why didn't we just...(*beat*) Oh, my God. Oh, God. You're leaving me aren't you?

BRIAN Maybe I wasn't clear enough.

MAY Oh, no, you were clear. You're leaving, I'm staying. That was very clear. Crystal clear. I just feel a little foolish that I didn't realize what was happening. It is happening, right?

BRIAN Yeah.

MAY   Yeah. Oh, boy. So, then it's not this country thing you can't live with. It's me.

BRIAN   May, please (*moving to coat, taking tie from jacket pocket and putting it on as they speak*)

MAY   Well, isn't it?

BRIAN   I just don't belong out here. All this open space. Seeing the same faces on the street every day. It's driving me nuts. People saying 'Hi' to you everywhere you go — like they know you.

MAY   They're being friendly.

BRIAN   Exactly! I can't stand it! I'm from the city for godssake! And then these people stop and talk to you, only they've got nothing to talk about. The weather. How many times a day can you talk about the damned weather?! I mean, in the city, nobody knows who you are and nobody cares. I know it sounds strange but, I find a certain measure of comfort in anonymity. Out here, it's like everybody knows everything about you. Every little detail.

MAY   Oh, Brian it's not like that at all.

BRIAN   It is. And money. Worrying about money all the time. Wondering if we can take it through the winter. I hate that. I've never had to do that before. I like a steady paycheck coming in.

MAY   Brian, it's our first year. It'll get better. We just have to be patient.

BRIAN   I don't want to be patient. I want it better now. Today. And then...and then there's you. My God, May.

MAY   What? What about me?

BRIAN   Well, look at you. Look what this place has done to you.

MAY   What?

BRIAN   Your appearance. You never dressed like that
             when we lived in the city. You wouldn't be
             caught dead looking like that.

MAY   Like what? What's wrong with the way I look?

BRIAN   What's wrong? You look like you're laying a
             railroad in Leningrad!

MAY   I'm going out to chop wood. What do you expect
             me to wear?

BRIAN   Well you don't have to dress like a farmer for
             godssake. It's like you don't care about yourself
             anymore. Like you just don't give a damn.

MAY   All right, so I'll put something strapless on.
             Then will you stay?

BRIAN   Don't joke. May. This is no time to joke.
             (*moving to get his jacket*) Now, I didn't have
             enough room for all of my clothes so I have to
             send for the rest later. And I'm taking the car too.
             I mean, I can't be making sales calls in a pick-up
             truck, now can I? And the car's got the phone
             too, and I need that, so...besides, the truck will
             be better for you out here anyway, especially in
             the winter.

MAY   All right, wait wait wait. This is all happening
             too fast. Can't we at least talk about this? I
             mean, you come in here, you spring this on me.
             We should talk about it.

BRIAN   There's no point, May. And besides, I don't have
             time. (*taking his overcoat from the coat stand*)

MAY   You don't have time?

BRIAN   No. I've got a meeting with John at one o'clock.

> *Angry, MAY grabs the overcoat from him and throws it on the floor.*

MAY

Damn it, Brian, I'm your wife! Don't tell me you don't have time. You had time to sit down and eat your goddamned breakfast! Don't I rate as much time as your bloody bacon and eggs?

BRIAN

May, I have a four-hour drive ahead of me. Did you expect me to make it without the bacon and eggs? (*turning and moving away, adjusting his tie*)

MAY

It's her again, isn't it?

BRIAN

Oh, here we go.

MAY

Of course it is. The clothes. The tie —

BRIAN

I told you, I have a meeting with John.

MAY

And who else are you meeting? Your little accountant friend with the big pair of portfolios?

BRIAN

I knew you'd bring her into it. I knew it.

MAY

Have you been talking to her?

BRIAN

Why does there always have to be another woman involved when a man leaves his wife? Huh? Can't you accept the fact that maybe, just maybe, a man has made decision in his life without being influenced by a woman?

MAY

Brian?

BRIAN

I talked to her once. Just once.

MAY

On the phone?

BRIAN

Yes.

MAY

You called her from here? On my phone?

BRIAN Yes. What the hell difference does it make where I called her from?

MAY It makes a big difference. If you want to call the tramp, you use your damned car phone. You don't use our phone in our own house. That's like bringing her into our bed.

BRIAN I used the car phone too, all right? Does that make it better?

MAY You said you only called her once.

BRIAN Right. Once from here and once from the car phone. And she's not a tramp.

MAY Oh? And what do you call a woman who sleeps with another woman's husband?

BRIAN She's headstrong.

MAY She's a mink!

BRIAN May, just drop it, all right.

MAY So, what did she say? Did she ask you to come back? Is that why you're leaving?

BRIAN I'm leaving for a lot of reasons. It's not just one thing, it's a lot of things...

MAY And she's one of them.

BRIAN Don't forget, it was your idea to move out here.

MAY Is she one of them?

BRIAN I told you I wasn't sure about it and yet I came. For you. To try and help the marriage. Well, it didn't work out.

MAY Is she one of the reasons?!

BRIAN   Yes! Honest to God, May, you're making this far
               more difficult than it has to be.

MAY   You're damn right I am!

BRIAN   Well, I would think that a woman with your
               intelligence would've seen this coming, so don't
               tell me this is a complete surprise to you.

MAY   Yes, it is. I thought we were happy out here.

BRIAN   You. You were happy out here. For me, it's been
               a struggle from day one.

MAY   Well, why didn't you tell me?

BRIAN   I did. Every bloody day. Every way I knew how.
               You just weren't listening.

MAY   You did no such thing.

BRIAN   Not with words. With my actions.

MAY   What actions? Like what?

BRIAN   I don't know, like...well, for instance when was
               the last time you saw me laugh. Huh? Or heard
               me say anything funny?

MAY   You never say anything funny.

BRIAN   Oh, yes I do.

MAY   No, you don't.

BRIAN   Yes, I do.

MAY   No, you don't.

BRIAN   If I have reason to, May, I can be every bit as
               funny as the next fellow. Every damned bit. I can
               be hilarious under the right circumstances.

MAY   So, that's what I should've noticed? You didn't
               tell jokes?

BRIAN   And don't belittle me either. I'm telling you what
               I think. I'm telling you my feelings. And what
               do you do? You make fun.

MAY   I thought that's what you wanted. More jokes.

BRIAN   Making fun is not jokes. Making fun is
               belittling a person. You, that's what you do. You
               belittle.

MAY   Do you love her?

BRIAN   Oh, that is so predictable.

MAY   Well?

BRIAN   Why do you want to know that? Why?

MAY   You told me before that you didn't. Were you
               lying to me?

BRIAN   No...

MAY   So, why are you leaving? Do you love her now?

BRIAN   May...

MAY   Just tell me.

BRIAN   May, please

MAY   It's all right. I'm a big girl. I can take it. And I
               mean, if you love her then maybe this'll all make
               sense. Now, do you love her or *not?*

BRIAN   (*beat*) Yes.

MAY   You bastard!

> *MAY punches BRIAN in the stomach and beats him over the back until he falls to his knees, then she kneels beside him.*

MAY   You lying, cheating, rotten, bastard! You should die for this, you pig!

> *MAY stops hitting BRIAN, and backs off.*

BRIAN   Well, you took that well. Good for you.

MAY   I'm sorry. (*near tears*)

BRIAN   (*still on his knees*) Don't be sorry. I mean, better to get it out now than to sit stewing about it. Right? (*as MAY doesn't answer*) Well...this is it then, I guess. (*getting to his feet*) I'm not sure what you say to a person at a time like this. I....this will be better for both of us, May.

MAY   No.

BRIAN   It will. You'll see. And moving out here actually did us some good. I mean, we both know where we belong now. You, out here with your friendly neighbours and your greater life expectancy, and me...anywhere else. I mean, you don't need me. What do you need me for? You do all the work around here. You run the business, you keep the books. I'm just an accessory. I complete the outfit. I'm the Little Boy Blue for your Bo Peep costume. (*beat*) I'm sorry. (*moving to pick up cases and coat*) Take care of yourself, and don't make me worry about you, you hear? (*starting for the door*)

MAY   I'll hate you, Brian. If you leave, I'll hate you, so help me I will.

BRIAN   (*beat*) Good-bye, May.

> *BRIAN exits. MAY is left alone on her knees. Lights down.*
>
> *End Act One, Scene One.*

Act One, Scene Two

	The time is about three weeks later. As the scene opens there is no one on stage. The pot of coffee is on the table. QUINN appears outside and looks into the house through the door U.C. He looks around for a moment, then knocks. There is a beat, and he knocks again.

MAY   (*off*) Just a minute!

QUINN opens the door and steps inside. He is a man in his mid-thirties although he looks older because of his unkempt condition. He carries a beaten old overnight bag.

QUINN   Hello? Hello? (*looking around*))

MAY enters on the stairs. She wears a housecoat now, and is somewhat unkempt in her own way and appears tired. She stops, looking slightly startled to discover QUINN there.

MAY   Yes?

QUINN   Did you say come in?

MAY   No, I said 'Just a minute'.

QUINN	Oh, sorry. (*turning to exit*)
MAY	Well, hold on.
QUINN	I thought you said come in, so...
MAY	Well, you're in now.
QUINN	Well, I can go back out.
MAY	No, no. Come in.
QUINN	No, I'll go out and knock again.
MAY	No, you don't have to do —
QUINN	Please, please. I'll feel better. This way I feel like I've intruded on you.
MAY	But, you haven't.
QUINN	But, I feel like I have. I'll just go out again. It's okay.

> *QUINN exits. MAY waits for a moment and there is no knock.*

| MAY | Well? |

> *QUINN enters again.*

QUINN	Well what?
MAY	Are you going to knock?
QUINN	Are you in a hurry?
MAY	Well, I'm standing here waiting.
QUINN	Oh, okay. Sorry.

> *QUINN exits again, then knocks.*

| MAY | Who is it? |

QUINN enters, smiling.

QUINN   That's a good one.

MAY   Do you feel better now?

QUINN   Yes. Thank you.

MAY   Good.

QUINN   I didn't wake you, did I?

MAY   No.

QUINN   I mean, it's eleven o'clock and you're still in your night clothes, so I thought...

MAY   I was just lying down.

QUINN   Ah. Feeling sick?

MAY   Well, I've been better.

QUINN   Yeah, you and me both. Oh, the name's Quinn. (*holding out his hand*)

MAY   (*shaking his hand*) Yes, I've seen you around town. May Henning.

QUINN   Pleased to meet you. I've seen you around too. You're the ones with the car phone.

MAY   Yes.

QUINN   Right. Pretty exciting stuff. (*moving and looking around*) So, you're the new owners here. (*studying the craftsmanship of the fireplace*) It's a beautiful place, Mrs. Henning. Beautiful. Built way back when workmanship was a thing of pride. Not like now. No, ma'am. Nowadays speed's the thing. Like an insatiable sailor in a whorehouse. Get it up quick and move on to the next one.

MAY	(*smiling politely*) Yes.
QUINN	You get much use out of that thing around here?
MAY	What thing?
QUINN	The car phone.
MAY	Oh. Well, not really, no.
QUINN	Didn't think so.
MAY	So, what can I help you with Mr. Quinn?
QUINN	Well, actually it's what I can help you with. You see...I wonder, is that coffee I smell?
MAY	Yes.
QUINN	(*beat, waiting for an invitation*) Are you saving it for anybody, or...
MAY	No. Would you...uh...would you like a cup?
QUINN	Ma'am, I'd love one right about now.
MAY	All right. Come and sit down. (*moving*)
QUINN	(*following*) Thank you. Thank you very much.
	MAY gets a cup from the china cabinet and pours coffee.
QUINN	Gettin' cold out there. I'd say we've got some weather comin' our way.
MAY	Could be.
QUINN	Yeah, wouldn't surprise me one bit to see a frost overnight. Damn near cold enough last night for one.
MAY	Really?

QUINN   Damn near.

MAY   There you go.

               *MAY sets the mug on the table, then
               pours a cup for herself.*

QUINN   Thank you. (*sitting, then pulling a mickey of
               whiskey from his coat, and unscrewing the top*)
               Ahhh. The first cup of the day is always the best
               one, isn't it? (*pouring whiskey into cup and
               speaking*) A little enhancement. Takes the edge
               off. You? (*holding bottle out to MAY*)

MAY   No, thank you.

QUINN   (*putting bottle back in coat.*) Oh. All right. You
               know, some people don't like to drink alone.
               Fortunately it's never bothered me a helluva lot. I
               guess I've kinda gotten used to it. (*taking a drink,
               then choking*) Decaf, right?

MAY   Yes.

QUINN   Shoulda warned me. (*taking bottle out and
               pouring more into cup*)

MAY   So, you had something you wanted to talk
               about?

QUINN   Well, yes. Now, I don't know whether you've
               heard or not but I had a...well, a little mishap
               last week with my motor home.

MAY   Yes, I heard. I'm sorry.

QUINN   Thank you. Stove blew up. I got out with the
               clothes on my back and this bag. Actually I
               never liked living there especially. It wasn't the
               best of situations. Particularly in the winter. I
               mean, somehow it just doesn't sit right, a man
               having to go out on a cold January morning to
               jump start his house. It was more a dwelling of
               convenience.

MAY	Convenience?
QUINN	(*getting up with coffee and looking the house over as he moves*) Yes, ma'am. You see, I'm afraid I'm a little short in the way of capital. Financially embarrassed as they say. So, anyway, since the fire, I've been living over in Frank Tucker's barn, but like I say, the nights are gettin' awfully cool now and that barn's got quite a draft. And, that's why I've come to you. You see, I know that you're in, well, kind of a tough spot yourself, I mean, what with your husband dumping you the way he did. So...
MAY	What?
QUINN	I'm sorry. Maybe that was a little indelicate of me.
MAY	My husband did not dump me.
QUINN	No?
MAY	No.
QUINN	I'm sorry. I heard he left.
MAY	Well, he left, yes, but, he just had to go back to the city on business, that's all.
QUINN	Business?
MAY	Yes. He's a salesman for an electronics company.
QUINN	I thought he quit that job.
MAY	Who told you that?
QUINN	Ronny Hall. The fella who runs the Esso station? Said he heard it from Les Judson over at the donut shop. Word is you and your husband both quit good jobs so's you could move out here and be a little closer to the poverty line.

MAY	We did not move out here to get closer to poverty. In fact, that's why my husband took his job back. Because...because we need the money.
QUINN	Oh. So, you expect him back then?
MAY	Well, yes.
QUINN	I see.
MAY	Sometime.
QUINN	You're not sure when?
MAY	Well, not completely no, but sometime.
QUINN	Uh-huh. So, your husband left, took a job in the city, and didn't say when he's coming back.
MAY	That's right.
QUINN	I don't know, Mrs. Henning, that sounds like being dumped to me.
MAY	Well, it's not.
QUINN	Fine. I'll take your word for it. Hard to imagine him coming back though, after what he said.
MAY	What he said?
QUINN	Well, he stopped for gas over at the Esso on his way out of town last week and Ronny Hall overheard him telling someone on his car phone that he was glad to be gettin' his ass out of this whistle stop. I guess he just meant that he was glad to be gettin' his ass out of here for a *while*.
MAY	Yes, that's all he meant.
QUINN	Right. Well, in the meantime, until he gets his ass back here, I was wondering if you might need some help around the place. I noticed a big stack of wood out there that needs to be split and I'm

QUINN   (*continued*) sure there must be a few other things you could use a hand with.

MAY   Well...

QUINN   I wouldn't be asking for any cash payment now. All I'd want is a room and maybe A good home-cooked meal every now and then. I mean, there's nothing like home-cooking on a crisp autumn night. My mother, she never let a night go by from October through to springtime without a hot meal for us.

MAY   You're from here are you?

QUINN   Born and raised. My father was the chief of police here at one time.

MAY   Oh, then you have family here?

QUINN   No, not any more.

MAY   They moved?

QUINN   They died.

MAY   Oh.

QUINN   They were thinkin' of movin', but, then they died.

MAY   I'm sorry.

QUINN   I know what you're getting at though. You're wonderin' if I have any relatives that'd take me in. Well, no ma'am I don't. And I don't have a whole lot of close friends nearby either. So, I guess that leaves you.

MAY   Well, Mr. Quinn...I mean, I do sympathize with you and your situation but...

QUINN   I'm harmless, if that's what you're worried about.

MAY   No, I wasn't...

QUINN   No, that's all right. I know that a woman living all alone has to be concerned about who she lets into her home, but you'll be safe with me. I guarantee it. You can ask Frank Tucker's cow. I've been sleeping with her for over a week now and I haven't laid a hand on her. Although God knows she's been askin' for it.

> *QUINN laughs a bit. MAY says nothing and QUINN sets his coffee down on the table.*

Well, that's okay. I can't say as I blame you really. I mean, a woman can't be too careful. I want to thank you for the coffee though. That was very nice of you. Very generous. (*moving to the door*)

MAY   (*standing*) Mr. Quinn? I guess I could use a hand with that wood. God knows I don't feel like doing it. And the back porch could use some mending too.

QUINN   There you go.

MAY   But it would only be for a while. I mean, probably just a week or two.

QUINN   Right. Until your husband comes back. The day he comes home, I'm gone. You can count on it.

MAY   Fine. You can have the room at the back. It's right through here.(*moving*) There's a bathroom on this floor too. That'll be yours.

QUINN   (*picking up his bag and following*). Good enough.

MAY   You know, I've got a cupboard in the kitchen that needs to be fixed too.

QUINN   Oh? What's the problem there?

MAY	Well, underneath the shelf. You know those little supports?
QUINN	The holdy thingys?
MAY	Right. One of them isn't holding properly.
QUINN	Well, I'll tell you what. You make up list of everything you want done and I'll get right to work.
MAY	All right, I'll do that. (*there is a knock on the door*) Just a minute!
QUINN	Thanks a lot Mrs. Henning. I really appreciate this.
MAY	Well, let's look at it as something that, hopefully, we'll both benefit from.

QUINN exits.

(*calling after QUINN*) It's the one at the end of the hall.

There is a knock at the door.

Coming.

MAY moves to open the door. HANK BEAVIS is standing there. He is dressed in a business suit and overcoat and he carries a briefcase . He is calling to someone on the street.

HANK	Morning, Roy! Cooled off real fast, didn't it? They're saying we might get a frost tonight! (*noticing MAY*) Oh, Mrs. Henning. Good morning.
MAY	Good morning.
HANK	Hank Beavis. From the bank?

MAY   Oh, yes, yes. I'm sorry. Come in, come in.

HANK   Thank you. (*entering*) Probably should've called before barging in like this.

MAY   (*closing the door*) Not at all. I was just having some coffee. Would you like some?

HANK   Well (*checking his watch*) I'm expected back at the bank shortly...oh, what the heck. Let's throw caution to the wind. Five minutes couldn't hurt, now could it.

MAY   All right.

HANK and MAY move to the table.

HANK   Chilly out there this morning. Winter's not too far off now I suppose.

MAY   No, I suppose not.

HANK   They're saying we might even get a frost tonight.

MAY   So I hear. Well, I guess we have to expect it sooner or later, don't we?

HANK   I guess we do. We can't stop the changing of the seasons now, can we? (*looking at her robe*) I didn't get you up, did I?

MAY   No.

HANK   (*looking at his watch*) I mean, it is eleven o'clock, and uh...(*pointing to her robe*) You're not sick, are you?

MAY   No, I just haven't bothered getting dressed yet, that's all.

HANK   I see. Been up and dressed since seven myself. Of
        course, I have to be at work for eight-thirty, and
        it makes a difference when you have someplace
        to get to I suppose, and you of course are going
        nowhere.

MAY   Yes. So, is this a social visit Mr. Business or are
        you here on Beavis? I mean...

HANK   That's all right. Actually, it's a little bit of both.
        You see, I was on my way back from the
        hospital and happened to be passing by so I
        thought I'd drop in. (*taking off his coat and
        sitting at the table*)

MAY   Hospital? (*taking a mug and pouring coffee for
        HANK*)

HANK   I was visiting a friend. Lucille Jorgensen. It's
        nothing serious. Just recovering from a little
        shock. She and her husband were trapped in the
        carwash last week. It's taking her a little time to
        get over it.

MAY   Oh, what a shame.

HANK   Yes. I don't think she'll ever be able to look at a
        can of Turtle Wax again. The car's never looked
        better though. I'd guess you could near about
        skate on that thing right now. Actually I'm more
        a friend of her husband Willy than I am Lucille.
        Willy and I played together on the high school
        basketball team years ago. We led the team to the
        championship in '71. Only championship the
        school's ever won. Willy and I were, well, kind
        of the team leaders I guess.

MAY   Oh, a star were you?

HANK   (*modestly*) Well, you know...(*looking around the
        house*) My, you certainly have done this house
        up nicely, Mrs. Henning. Quite nicely indeed.
        Makes me feel all the prouder that the bank was

HANK	(*continued*) able to help you out on the mortgage end of things.
MAY	(*setting the mug down*) Here we go.
HANK	Thank you. (*noticing the mug*) Oh, that's a lovely mug. Yes, very nice. You didn't buy it here, did you?
MAY	(*sitting down*) Well, as a matter of fact, no.
HANK	Mexico?
MAY	No.
HANK	Cuba?
MAY	No.
HANK	Honduras?
MAY	No. British Isles?
HANK	Oh, Scotland.
MAY	No.
HANK	England?
MAY	No.
HANK	Wales?
MAY	No.
HANK	Ireland?
MAY	Yes.
HANK	(*excited*) I knew it. Uncanny, isn't it? You're probably wondering how I guessed.
MAY	(*pointing to the mug*) The shamrock?

HANK   (*looking at the mug*) Oh, no, no. You see it's
         kind of a hobby with me. Collecting mugs. At
         last count we had seven hundred and nineteen at
         home. Mother and I. She's a collector too. You
         know, you'd be surprised at how much you can
         tell about a person just by looking at their mugs.

MAY   (*smiling, feigning interest*) Really?

HANK   Oh, yes. You can tell whether or not they have a
         sense of humour, if they do a lot of travelling,
         what their politics are. Any number of
         characteristics.

MAY   All from mugs.

HANK   Fascinating isn't it?

MAY   (*affirmatively*) Oh.

HANK   Mugging, we call it. The practice of collecting
         and studying mugs. I suppose that would make
         us muggers (*laughing as MAY laughs politely*)
         That's sort of a running joke between Mother and
         I. Muggers. I mean, if you could see Mother.
         She's just a little bitty thing.

MAY   So, you live with your mother do you?

HANK   Yes, ma'am. You probably find that strange,
         right? A man my age living with his mother.
         You probably think I'm...you know.

MAY   Gay?

HANK   No!

MAY   Oh.

HANK   I was going to say a mama's boy.

MAY   Oh, right.

HANK   But, I'm not.

MAY   Of course not.

HANK   No, the truth is, Mother's not well and I'm the only one she's got, so...

MAY   I see. So, Mr. Beavis, you said this was sort of a business visit?

HANK   Oh, yes. Well, the thing is Mrs. Henning, we at the bank have made it a point over the years to genuinely care about our customers. It's not just good business with us, it's...well, I like to think it's more a way of life. Caring. Looking out for our neighbours as it were. And...well, I must admit our concern for you is running a little high right about now.

MAY   Oh? Why's that?

HANK   Well, this...this business with your husband.

MAY   My husband?

HANK   Yes. His deserting you the way he did. You see —

MAY   Wait a minute, wait. Who told you my husband deserted me?

HANK   Well, I've heard it from a number of people. Um, Ronny Hall, the fellow who runs the —

MAY & HANK   Esso Station.

HANK   Yes, I heard it from him.

MAY   He must be giving this information away free with every fill-up, is he?

HANK   Well, that's our Ronny. Actually, the first person I heard it from was Christine Wurtz, one of our tellers. She was the one who waited on your husband when he withdrew the money.

MAY	Withdrew what money?
HANK	Well, the day he left, he came in and withdrew some money from your joint account. That was when he told Christine that if he never saw this backwoods arse-pick of a town again, it'd be too soon. Now, perhaps we jumped to the wrong conclusion but we took that to mean he wasn't, coming back.
MAY	How much money?
HANK	Beg your pardon?
MAY	The withdrawal. How much did he take?
HANK	Well, as I recall, it was thirty-four hundred dollars. You mean you didn't know?
MAY	Of course I knew. I just forgot the exact amount, that's all.
HANK	Yes. Well, I just want you to know that the bank is there for you. If you find yourself short over the off-season as many of our merchants do, this being mainly a resort town, then please don't hesitate to call on us.
MAY	Thirty-four hundred?
HANK	Yes.
MAY	(*to herself*) Son of a bitch. (*getting up and moving*)
HANK	He didn't like it here, did he?
MAY	(*lost on thought*) Hmm?
HANK	Your husband. More the city type wasn't he?
MAY	Yes. I suppose.
HANK	Yes. Do you know how I knew?

MAY   (*beat*) Mugs?

HANK   No. no, this has got nothing to do with mugs. You see, in your husband I recognized a kindred spirit. I'm the same way. The city's in my blood. In fact, I'd be there right now if it weren't for Mother's health. I mean, the bank's been after me for a couple of years now to move up and manage one of their bigger branches, but with Mother, well...It's funny, isn't it, how our direction in life is often charted by someone else? (*beat*) So, he has left you then?

MAY   Uh...well, just temporarily. He has business in the city and we thought this might be a good time for a little vacation from one another. That's all it is.

HANK   Oh, I see. And when do you expect him back?

MAY   Well, I'm not sure. Soon.

HANK   So, it's not a permanent arrangement then.

MAY   No, not at all.

HANK   Oh. Then I suppose you wouldn't be entertaining thoughts of going out with someone if they were to ask.

MAY   Going out?

HANK   Yes. You know, just going out for an evening.

MAY   You mean on a date?

HANK   Well, I don't know if I'd put it as strongly as that, you being married and all. I'd say it'd be more like just going out, like you would if you went out by yourself, only you wouldn't be by yourself.

MAY   Who would I be with?

HANK	Whoever you like. Whoever asked you.
MAY	Nobody's asked me.
HANK	Ah. Well, in that case you would be by yourself. (*beat*) Of course, if you wanted some company, I could go along.
MAY	Well, that's very nice of you, but...
HANK	As a matter of fact, the annual Halloween dance is coming up at the Oddfellows and I happen to know that you've got a Little Bo Peep costume that might be going to waste.
MAY	You happen to know...
HANK	Yes. Mrs. Provich over at the fabric shop told me.
MAY	Mrs. Provich.
HANK	Yes, she said you were in to buy the material a couple of weeks ago. So, I figured as long as you've got the costume made, and I'm not going with anybody anyway, what the heck, why not go with you?
MAY	Well, you flatter me, but I don't think I feel like going to the dance any more.
HANK	Well, now I thought you might feel that way, but you know, at a time like this, with your husband deser...you know...away on business, you really shouldn't be alone. You should be with friends. And besides, it would be a shame to waste that costume after all the work you've put into it.
MAY	Well
HANK	Come on.
MAY	No. I don't think —

HANK	Oh, come on.
MAY	No.
HANK	It'll be fun.
MAY	No.
HANK	(*almost hurt*) You could at least think about It.
MAY	(*beat*) All right. I'll think about it.
HANK	That's the ticket. (*moving to get his coat*)
MAY	Give me a couple of days. I'll let you know in plenty of time so that if I decide not to go, then you can ask someone else.
HANK	There is no one else.
MAY	Oh.
HANK	I mean, you're the closest thing Grogan's Cove has to a single woman right now. You and the widow Perkins, and I wouldn't want to take her. I mean, she'd probably wind up getting drunk and making passes at all the married men. She's kind of a, if you'll pardon my French, tart.
MAY	I see.

QUINN enters.

QUINN	Mrs. Henning, I'm gonna get started or that wood now...(*noticing HANK*) Well, well, well. Hi, Hank.
HANK	(*coldly*) Quinn.
QUINN	Sorry. I didn't mean to interrupt anything.
MAY	Oh, you aren't interrupting. We were just talking about the Halloween dance.

QUINN	Oh. Goin' with the widow Perkins again this year, Hank?
HANK	Uh no. No.
QUINN	I heard she was the life of the party last year.
HANK	Yes, that's what I heard too!
MAY	Have you two known each other long?
HANK	I only went out with her that once. It's not like we were an item or anything.
MAY	No no no. I meant you and Mr. Quinn.
QUINN	Oh, yes, ma'am. Henry and I have quite a history. Isn't that right, Henry? We've known each other since we were what, five? Went all through public school together, high school. Built a tree house together in grade six, remember? God. Whatever happened to that?
HANK	Charlie Boyle and Garth Vogan chopped it down.
QUINN	Go on! They did not.
HANK	No, they did.
QUINN	I don't remember that.
HANK	Well, you weren't in it at the time.
QUINN	Oh. (*to MAY*) You see, I told you we had a history. (*to HANK*) Oh, and then there was Penny Hermitage.
MAY	Who's Penny Hermitage?
HANK	(*to MAY*) She's nobody. She...

QUINN   She's a girl I stole from Hank back in high
        school. Cute little English girl who moved here
        with her mother in what was it, Hank, grade
        twelve?

HANK   I really don't remember.

QUINN   Sure you do. It was the year we won the high
        school basketball championship.

MAY   Oh, you were on that team?

QUINN   Yeah, me and Henry both. Henry here was the
        best towel boy in the league. I mean, you went
        to the bench, Hank had that towel around your
        neck before your behind hit the pine. So, at the
        team party that year, Hank shows up with Penny
        on his arm. Of course, that surprised the rest of
        us because we never thought of Henry as being
        much of a ladies man. No offense, Henry, but
        let's face it, you didn't cut nearly as dashing
        figure back then as you do now. (*starting to
        laugh*) I mean, back in high school you were into
        collecting mugs. You were kind of dull. (*to
        MAY*) No, to make a long story short, Penny
        comes to the party with Hank here, but she
        leaves with me. You know, I've always felt bad
        about that, Hank.

HANK   No need for that. I barely remember it.

MAY   So, what happened to her?

QUINN   Who?

MAY   The girl. Is she still around?

QUINN   Uh, no. She moved away that spring.

HANK   Yes, her mother got herself involved in very
        messy situation hereabouts and had to leave
        town. Isn't that right, Quinn?

QUINN	(*a little uneasy*) Right. (*to MAY*) Well, I'd better get at that wood. Excuse me. (*moving*)
MAY	The axe is in the shed out there.
QUINN	I'll find it. (*exiting through the kitchen*)
HANK	Is he working for you?
MAY	Yes. Well, he's just helping out until my husband gets back.
HANK	So, the prodigal son returns.
MAY	Oh, he's been away has he?
HANK	From this house he has. His family used to own this place. He grew up in this house. I hope you know what you're doing, May, hiring him like that. I mean, I don't want to appear meddlesome but Quinn can be an odd one at times.
MAY	Oh, I don't know. He seems all right. And it's only for a couple of weeks.
HANK	Yes, well, as long as you're comfortable with it. (*checking his watch*) Oh, I'd better scoot. I have a meeting in ten minutes. (*moving to the door*)
MAY	Well, thank you for stopping by. I appreciate your concern.
HANK	Not at all. And don't forget what I said about the bank now. We're there for you if you need us.
MAY	I'll keep that in mind.
HANK	And you'll let me know about the Halloween dance?
MAY	Yes. Yes, I will.

HANK	Good. I'll keep my fingers crossed. (*starting to exit, then returning*) You know, maybe we could get together some night for a game of Scrabble.
MAY	Scrabble?
HANK	Yes, I'm the president of the new Scrabble Club. We meet Wednesdays. Maybe you could join us one night.
MAY	Scrabble. Well, if I can free up some time I'll certainly keep that in mind.
HANK	Good. Well, gotta run. Have a good day now.
MAY	Good-bye.

HANK exits.

HANK	(*off*) Morning, Wendel! Cold enough for you?
MAY	Yikes.

MAY moves to the table and picks up the mugs. QUINN enters. He is carrying one piece of wood. He moves to the fireplace. MAY exits to the kitchen. QUINN sets the wood down.

QUINN	That's one. (*taking bottle from pocket and drinking*)

MAY enters from kitchen.

MAY	Oh, Mr. Quinn?
QUINN	It's just Quinn, ma'am. No mister.
MAY	You didn't tell me you used to live in this house.
QUINN	Didn't think it was important. Is it?
MAY	Well, no, it's just that - I don't know - I thought you might've told me.

QUINN   That was a long time ago, Mrs. Henning. So
         long ago it seems like I never lived here at all. I
         guess that's why I didn't mention it.

MAY   Oh. Well, how does...I mean, excuse me for
         asking this, but how does a police chief's son go
         from living in a home like this to....

QUINN   No home at all? Well, it wasn't by design. You
         see, my parents died when I was seventeen and
         the house had to be sold to pay off the creditors,
         so, I moved into Betty Granger's Boarding
         House, started picking up odd jobs here and there
         and...well, before you know it, here I am. Gone
         from a better place.

MAY   What happened? To your parents I mean.

QUINN   My mother was taken by a heart attack. My
         father was shot.

MAY   Oh, God. I'm sorry, Quinn. I didn't...

QUINN   Oh, don't be sorry. Like I said, it was a long
         time ago. Besides, you don't need to be worryin'
         about my problems. You've got enough of your
         own.

MAY   Yes, but...(*then defensive*)...what
         problems? I don't have any problems.

QUINN   No?

MAY   No.

QUINN   Well, if you say so. (*starting to leave*)

MAY   You've got more problems than I do.

QUINN   You think so?

MAY   Definitely. Way more. I mean, at least I've got a
         home. You've got no home, no money, no
         steady job, no family. You've got nothing.

QUINN   Gee, I didn't realize how bad off I was. Thank you.

MAY   No, I didn't mean for it to sound that way.

QUINN   That's all right. That's the way it is.

MAY   All I meant was, don't feel bad for me. Because if I did have any problems, which I don't, they wouldn't be anything I couldn't handle. I mean, nobody likes a good challenge more than me. If there's a problem to take care of or work to be done, then I'm there. Like a rock. All right?

QUINN   Fine.

MAY   Fine.

QUINN   Now, what do you say we get at that wood?

MAY   What do you mean we?

QUINN   Well, I noticed there's two axes out there.

MAY   So?

QUINN   So, you likin' a good challenge the way you do, I thought maybe you'd like to pitch in.

MAY   Oh. Well...uh...all right, sure.

QUINN   Good. Besides, a little physical activity might take your mind off your problems.

MAY   I don't have any problems!

QUINN   Oh. Sorry. I forgot. (*with a bit of a smirk*) Well, see you out there.

MAY   What are you smirking about?

QUINN   I'm not smirking.

MAY   Yes, you are. You're smirking.

QUINN	Well, I don't feel like I'm smirking.
MAY	Well, you are.
QUINN	Well, then it must be one of those subconscious smirks. The kind that sneak up on you.
MAY	You think this is funny?
QUINN	Think what's funny?
MAY	This. Me. My problems.
QUINN	You don't have any problems.
MAY	You're damn right I don't.
QUINN	Fine.
MAY	The only problem I have is you people thinking I've got problems.
QUINN	Yes, ma'am.
MAY	And please don't call me ma'am. My name is May.
QUINN	May it is.
MAY	Good. Any other problems?
QUINN	None. You?
MAY	Not one.
QUINN	Good.
MAY	And the next time you see Ronny Hall you can tell him that for me!

QUINN   Oh, I wouldn't worry about what Ronny Hall says. Nobody pays much attention to him anyway. I mean, the man can't count to twenty-one unless he's buck naked.

> *QUINN exits. Light down.*

> *End of Act One, Scene Two.*

Act One, Scene Three

>*The time is three weeks later. The night of the Halloween dance. As the scene opens MAY and HANK are returning from the Halloween dance. MAY enters wearing her Little Bo Peep outfit, complete with staff and a stuffed lamb She has had a little too much to drink, leaving her slightly tipsy. The wood box near the fireplace is full now.*

MAY   Quinn? Yoo-hoo? Anybody home? (*calling to HANK outside*) It's all clear, Hank.

>*HANK enters in a bunny costume carrying a big papier maché or styrofoam carrot on a string around his neck. MAY leans her staff against the wall as HANK moves and opens the kitchen door cautiously to check for QUINN.*

I don't know what you're worried about. I mean, so what if Quinn sees you?

HANK   Oh, if he saw me like this I'm sure he'd make some sort of wise crack.

MAY   Well, anyway thank you for a wonderful evening, Hanker. (*shaking his hand*) It was just the lift I needed. Drive carefully.

HANK   What, you're sending me home already?

MAY   Well, it's late.

HANK   But, you promised me a glass of cognac, remember?

MAY   I did?

HANK   You sure did. As we were leaving the dance. You also promised me a quick game of Scrabble. You mean you've forgotten already?

MAY   Certainly not! Forgotten. You shall have your cognac sir, and your Scrabble too, or my name isn't Little Be Pope.

> *MAY hands HANK her lamb, goes to the cabinet and pulls out a bottle of cognac. Then she gets a glass out of the cabinet and pours HANK a drink. He follows.*

HANK   So. That was a lot of fun tonight, huh? (*setting the lamb on the table*)

MAY   Oh, yes. Those Oddfellows are a bunch of odd fellows, that's for sure.

HANK   Well, they throw a Jim Dandy party, you can bet on that. They have an annual Christmas party too. Say, what say you and I go to that one together too?

MAY   Well, that's a long way off yet.

HANK   December nineteenth. I could pick you up about eight.

MAY   Well, let's just wait and see, shall we? (*handing him the glass of cognac*) There you go. One cognac for the gentleman in the fur coat.

HANK   You're not going to join me?

MAY   Oh no, I think I'm over my limit. I'm starting to
              see giant mammals. (*laughing and slapping
              HANK on the arm*)

HANK   Just one more. Here. (*taking a glass out for
              MAY*)

MAY   No, I couldn't, really.

HANK   (*taking the bottle and pouring a glass*)) What, not
              even one drink with a friend? I mean, we are
              friends, aren't we?

MAY   Sure, we're friends.

HANK   Well, friend?

MAY   Oh, all right.

HANK   That's the idea, May.

MAY   But just the one.

HANK   Absolutely. You know, that's a pretty name,
              May. Were you born in May? (*handing her the
              glass*)

MAY   June.

HANK   Oh.

MAY   My sister April was born in May. (*moving*)
              Now, where did I put that Scrabble game?
              (*exiting to hallway*)

HANK   (*smoothing costume and straightening his ears*)
              You know, the Grogan's Cove High alumni are
              playing a basketball game in the school gym
              tomorrow night.

MAY   (*entering with Scrabble game*) Yes, I heard. How
              nice for the little hoopsters. (*sitting at the table*)

HANK	Yes, and they're going to be honoring the '71 team at half time. The championship team? So, anyway, they're making a big to-do about it, giving us medals and everything and...well, I was wondering if you'd want to go. With me I mean.
MAY	Oh, I don't know, Hank
HANK	(*sitting at the table*) It'd sure be great to have you there. Most of the other guys have got wives and kids, and they'll be there cheering them on, but I don't have anyone like that.
MAY	What about your Mother?
	They begin setting up the game.
HANK	Oh no, the excitement might be too much for her. Besides, her wrestling's on t.v. tomorrow night and she doesn't like to miss that.
MAY	Well...
HANK	You don't have to give me an answer right now. Tomorrow'll be soon enough. All right? Will you think about it?
MAY	All right.
HANK	Good. (*beat*) Tell me something, May. How do you....how do you feel about small-town fellas?
MAY	Oh, I don't know. I mean, small town, big city. Men can be jerks no matter where they're from.
HANK	Well, what if you met a small town fella who wasn't a jerk?
MAY	Oh, I've met a few who seem nice. You, Quinn.
HANK	You think Quinn's nice?
MAY	Sure. He's nice to me.

HANK	Well, if you want a friend's advice, I think you should give him a wide berth.
MAY	Why?
HANK	Because he can only lead to trouble.
MAY	Well, he has had it pretty rough though, hasn't he? I mean, his mother dying and then his father going the way he did. That must've been awful.
HANK	I suppose.
MAY	How did it happen? Was it a hold-up or something?
HANK	What?
MAY	Quinn's father.
HANK	Quinn's father? Quinn's father shot himself in the head.
MAY	What?
HANK	You didn't know? It was a couple of days after Mrs. Quinn's funeral. The Chief drove his patrol car out to the gravel pit and bang.
MAY	Oh, God.
HANK	Oh, the Quinn family was in the papers for weeks. (*going to cabinet and pouring himself another drink*) You see, Chief Quinn was having this affair with Penny's mom. We told you about Penny. The little English girl? Well, pretty soon everybody was on to them. The city council was even asking Chief Quinn to resign over it. Well, that's why Penny's mom left town. It got to be too much for her. It was too much for Mrs. Quinn too, I guess. Her heart gave out.

HANK moves back to the table and sits.

MAY   Oh, my God. (*getting up and moving*)

HANK   Nice woman too, Mrs. Quinn. So, anyway,
               that's it. Everything you need to know about
               Quinn. Now, why don't we get on to a more
               pleasant topic? Hmm? Let's talk about...well,
               let's talk about you and me?

MAY   (*only half listening*) Hmm?

HANK   You and me. Us.

MAY   What about us?

HANK   Well, I mean, here we are, all alone, a moonlit
               night, fine cognac, costumes. I think we'd be
               fools not to seize the moment, don't you?

MAY   Seize what moment?

HANK   (*standing*) This one. The one that destiny has lead
               us to.

               HANK moves in on MAY who moves
               back.

MAY   I thought you wanted to play Scrabble?

HANK   I'm very attracted to you. May. Very attracted.

MAY   Well, I like you too, Hank. Up to a point.

HANK   May, I want you.

MAY   And that's the point.

HANK   Please, May. I've wanted you since the first day
               we met.

MAY   What?

HANK   I want to...I want to love you. Oh, May...

> *HANK backs MAY into the table. He*
> *embraces her and kisses her neck.*

MAY	(*in pain*) Oh, Hank.
HANK	(*passion*) Oh, May.
MAY	Hank, please. Your carrot.
HANK	Don't rush it May, all in good time.
MAY	Dammit, Hank. (*pushing him away and holding up the carrot*) God. It was digging into my ribs. (*moving away*)
HANK	Oh, I'm sorry.
MAY	What do you think you're doing anyway?
HANK	I'm making a play for you. (*moving in again*)
MAY	Well, don't.
HANK	May, please. If I don't take my shot now, somebody's gonna beat me to it.
MAY	Hank, stop it.
HANK	Come, let's perform pagan acts together.
MAY	Stop it, Hank, right now! (*having been chased around to the table again and now leaning against it*)
HANK	(*getting up*) What? What is it? It's the bunny suit, right? Huh? I knew that was a mistake. I knew it. I should've gone with the gladiator. Well, just ignore the costume. (*leaping at her and landing on her on the table*)
MAY	Get off me!
HANK	Let me love you, May.

MAY	Hank, no!
HANK	I want to be unbridled. I want to satisfy my thirst for depravity.
	QUINN enters . Wearing a bathrobe and is clean-shaven now. He looks at the two of them on the table. They don't see him.
QUINN	What's up Doc?
	HANK freezes, then jumps to his feet.
HANK	Quinn. What are you doing here?
QUINN	Well, as luck would have it, I was about to satisfy a thirst too. (*moving to the cabinet*) I hope you don't mind, Mrs. Henning, but I was gonna borrow a snifter of your brandy. I'll replace it tomorrow, I promise. (*there is a brief pause as he takes out the bottle and pours himself a drink*) So, how was the dance, kids?
HANK	Ah fine. Fine. We were just...saying goodnight.
QUINN	What, hittin' the bunny trail already?
HANK	(*to MAY*) I told you. Didn't I tell you?
QUINN	I must say, Mrs. Henning, you surprise me. Bringing home a piece of fluff like this.
HANK	See? Well...goodnight.(*making his way to the door*) Thanks for the drink. And for the evening. And...well, thanks.
QUINN	Where you off to, Hank? Gonna do a little bar hopping?
HANK	All right that's it. You think you're funny, don't you Quinn? Huh? Well you wanna know what I think? (*moving closer to QUINN*)

QUINN   I'm all ears.

HANK   I think you're just like your old man was. You're
               a scar on this town's good name. And I think
               we'd all be a helluva lot better off without you.
               (*moving to the door and exiting*)

QUINN   (*to MAY*) Bunnies. Can't live with 'em, can't
               live without 'em. Listen, maybe you should call
               it a night.

MAY   What, you mean you don't want a turn?

QUINN   (*stopping*) Hmm?

MAY   Don't you wanna take a shot too? (*opening her
               arms in mock invitation*)

QUINN   No, I just wanted some brandy. Helps me sleep.

MAY   Oh, come on. I'm a woman. I'm all alone. I must
               need a man, right? So, come on, let's go.

QUINN   (*looking at MAY for a moment*) No, not with
               someone out of a nursery rhyme. I think that'd
               mess me up.

MAY   Come on. Here, I'll make it easy for you. (*taking
               her Little Bo Peep petticoat off, under which she
               is wearing frilly bloomers*) I'll save you the
               trouble of having to fake your way through any
               silly romantic foreplay. I mean, who needs
               romance, right? Empty promises born of an
               overripe libido, that's all romance is. So the hell
               with it. We'll just skip right to the bump and
               grind. (*the petticoat is off now*) There you go.
               Come and get it!

QUINN   You know, I do like it when you play hard to get
               like that.

MAY   Come on. This is what you want isn't it? See? That's what you all want. (*pointing to his crotch*) I mean, that...that thing is like a flag to you men. You raise it first thing in the morning, salute it all day long, and don't take it down until somebody blows taps over it.

QUINN   Yeah, we're a patriotic lot.

MAY   And you think that just because a woman's husband is away for a while, you think it's open season. I mean, you just want to pounce. You're always pouncing. Don't you think there should be more to it than that? Like feelings? God forbid maybe even love?

QUINN   I wouldn't know.

MAY   Exactly. None of you know. Your brain's in your ass and your heart's in your groin.

QUINN   Look, Mrs. Henning, you're talking to the wrong man when it comes to sex and love. The last woman I had was eight years ago. A tourist, I didn't know her name, grabbed me out of Kelty's Bar, took me to a boat down at the wharf and it was all over in about two minutes. Right there on the deck. Turns out she was gettin' her husband back for puttin' the make on a younger girl. I was twenty-seven at the time. The woman was close to fifty. It wasn't for love and it wasn't for lust and it sure as hell wasn't for long. And when it was over, she cried. I didn't know what to do, so I just left her there and went back to the bar. Her husband was still there. Still workin' on this other girl. He hadn't even missed us. So, don't go askin' me about love, because there's an awful lot about it that I don't understand. My only experience is that sometimes people get punished for it. And as for the rest of the men, well, I wouldn't go judging the whole lot of us on one or two. We're not all like your husband.

MAY   What's my husband got to do with it?

QUINN	Well, he's the one you're mad at, isn't he?
MAY	No.
QUINN	He's not?
MAY	No. All right, yes. Yes, I'm mad at him. I hate him for this. Making me do to that dance without him. All the men sizing me up. Looking at me like I was the hot new prospect in town. And the women. They used to talk to me, right to my face, when I had a husband nearby. Now, all I get are stares from across the room and whispers behind the hands. So, you're goddamn right I'm mad at him. (*near tears*) And when he gets back here, I'm gonna let him know that.
QUINN	(*beat*) So what was it? Another woman?
MAY	What?
QUINN	Your husband. Is that why he left?
MAY	No. Of course not.
QUINN	I mean, that's what usually turns a woman into a man-hater.
MAY	What makes you think I'm a man-hater?
QUINN	Brains in the ass. Heart in the groin. Call it a guess.
MAY	Well, I'm *not.* And my husband hasn't left me. How many times do I have to tell you people?! (*crying quietly*)
QUINN	(*not sure what to do*) Well, it's gettin' late. Maybe I should turn in. (*beat*) What about you, you tired? (*as MAY shakes her head no*) No, huh? Well! Actually neither am I? So, how 'bout a game of Scrabble?

MAY   No thanks.

QUINN   Sure, come on. One game. It's good for taking your mind off your problems. (*as MAY gives him a look*) If you had any problems. (*beat*) All right then, do it for me. You remember all those problems I've got? Huh? (*beat*) I'll let you go first.

MAY   Oh, all right.

QUINN   There you go. (*sitting back and picking out tiles*)

MAY   (*pointing at his robe*) Wait a minute. Isn't that my husband's robe?

QUINN   Oh, right. I hope you don't mind. It was hanging on the door in the bathroom down here and I took the liberty. I'll put it back if you...

MAY   Oh, don't worry about it. Wear it whenever you want. In fact, you're about his size so if you want to, you can go through his clothes upstairs and pick out whatever you like. They're in some boxes in the front bedroom.

QUINN   That wouldn't bother him?

MAY   No, of course not. He...he's not coming back, all right? And yes there is another woman. Satisfied?

QUINN   Look, I didn't mean to...

MAY   No, it's all right. (*putting some tiles on the board*) I don't know who I thought I was kidding anyway. That's why we moved out here in the first place. He was seeing this other woman. This...this home permanent with legs up to her chin. Slut. Eight points.

QUINN   Pardon me?

MAY   (*pointing to the board*) Slut. Double word. Eight points.

QUINN   Oh, very good. (*writing down her score*)

MAY   So then one day I get a phone call from a jewelry store wanting to know how to spell Miranda for the inscription on the bracelet. Well, naturally I confronted Brian and he confessed to having been seeing this Miranda for a couple of months but he promised to break it off. (*moving to the cabinet to pour another cognac*) That's when I talked him into moving away from the city. Out of sight, out *of* mind? So much for that old saw. So, that's it. He thinks he's in love with her now and he's not coming back. I was just afraid to admit it. And the funny thing is, I'm not even sure I loved him all these years. Yeah. I mean, we're not even that compatible. I like loud music in the morning. He likes Sinatra. I like the country. He likes the city. I like to make love with the lights on. He likes to make love with somebody else. But, even with all that was wrong, I didn't want to lose him. And if he came back tomorrow, after all this, I'd probably take him back.

QUINN   Why?

MAY   Why?

QUINN   Yeah, why?

MAY   (*beat*) Because I put some value in nine years of marriage? Because I'd hate to think that that was time wasted? I don't know. Because I'm weak? God, I can't believe I feel so bad about this. He...you know what he did? He sat down and ate breakfast before he broke the news to me. Yeah. Just sat there calmly, asked me to pass the salt, then left me. That was It. And then he goes to the bank and...well, the hell with him. I'm glad he's gone. No, I am. I'm better off without him. Much better. Did you hear that, Brian? (*going to the door and yelling*)That little strumpet can have you! She can have your Sinatra and your car phone and your lousy sex!

MAY   (*continued*) (*closing the door and turning to QUINN*) It was too, you know. The sex? It wasn't good at all. And not because of me. I mean, I was in there plugging. No, the problem was Brian. I don't know why exactly...

QUINN   (*finished putting his tiles in place*) Tiny.

MAY   Well, tinyish.

QUINN   Nine. (*marking his score*)

MAY   Hmn?

QUINN   Nine points. Tiny. I've got the triple letter here.

MAY   Oh. (*moving back to table*) Oh, and the car phone? That wasn't even his. He gave it to me for Christmas last year. And now he's got that too. (*putting some tiles down*) But, hey, why not? He's got everything else, right? He's got his little Miranda, and his car, and his high-paying job. (*beat*) Of course, I suppose if he's really in love with her I shouldn't hold it against him. I'd like to think I'm above that.

QUINN   (*looking at her word*) I think there are two T's in buttface.

MAY   Fourteen. Mark it down.

QUINN   (*marking the score*) You know, if you don't mind my saying so, self-pity isn't gonna help you any.

MAY   What?

QUINN   Feeling sorry for yourself. It's not gonna solve anything.

MAY   I'm not feeling sorry for myself.

QUINN   Oh, I think you are.

MAY   Oh, do you?

QUINN	Yes ma'am.
MAY	Well, why don't you let me worry about that?
QUINN	Ma'am, your husband's been gone how long now? A month? And you've been lying in that same pool of blood ever since. I mean, I'm tellin' you, self-pity might seem like a comfort to you, but it's not gonna get you back on your feet.
MAY	Yes, well, I guess you should know, shouldn't you? I mean, you're a prime example of what self-pity can do to a person?
QUINN	I'm sorry ma'am. I don't understand.
MAY	And you can knock off that rube act too. You might be able to fool everyone else in this town with your quaint little 'aw shucks' routine, but not me. I get the feeling you've got a lot more on the ball than you'd like us to believe.
QUINN	How's that?
MAY	Well, for instance, that bag you brought with you when you moved in. I took a look inside that bag the first day you were here.
QUINN	You went through my things?
MAY	Well, like you said, a woman can't be too careful. And you know what I found? Books. Mark Twain, Hemingway, Steinbeck. Now, what kind of man stops to collect his books when his trailer is burning down around him? Certainly not the kind of man you're making out to be. So, what is it? Are you ashamed of who you are? Ashamed of your family?
QUINN	You just never mind about my family, Mrs. Henning. I don't see where that's any of your business. And I'll ask you politely to please stay away from my things from now on.

MAY	Now, just a minute
QUINN	I'm asking you politely Mrs. Henning. Please do me the favour of respecting my request.
MAY	(*beat, rather reluctantly*) All right, I'm sorry.
QUINN	Fine.
MAY	And I'm sorry about bringing your family into it too. That was a cruel thing to say. It's just that I...I'm not having a good month, all right?
QUINN	Fine. Forget it.
MAY	And what I said before? About you wanting sex? I'm sorry about that too. I know you're not all sex maniacs. I mean, if anybody should be one, it's you.
QUINN	Come again?
MAY	You know, a man who hasn't had it in eight years.
QUINN	Oh. Right.
MAY	I'll tell you though, if I'd known that about you before, I probably wouldn't have let you stay here.
QUINN	Oh? (*putting some tiles down*)
MAY	Well, I mean, going that long without...and then being in a house with a woman who's all alone. You've shown great restraint.
QUINN	Thank you. Horny. Twenty-four. (*marking score*)
MAY	Of course, maybe it hasn't been that big a task for you?
QUINN	What?

MAY	Resisting the temptation to come on to me.
QUINN	A lot tougher than turnin' down Frank Tucker's cow.

They both smile.

MAY	You've got a nice sense of humour, you know that? I mean, most men take themselves so seriously these days. But you, you're different. (*putting some tiles down*)
QUINN	Could be because I've got nothing worth bein' serious about. I'm not sure whether that's good or bad.
MAY	Well, I like it. Arouse. Seven.
QUINN	Arouse?
MAY	Arouse.

QUINN marks the score.

MAY	So, is it hard?
QUINN	(*breaking his pencil*) Ma'am?
MAY	To resist the temptation. I mean, on a scale of one to ten, how hard am I to resist? Frank Tucker's cow being number one.
QUINN	Actually Frank's cow's about a three. But, you, you're way up there all right. I mean, well...there've been moments.
MAY	What moments?
QUINN	(*putting some tiles down*) Well, you know. Moments when I'd look at you, and...
MAY	Yes?

QUINN	Well, like that first day I was here and we were out splittin' the wood. And your cheeks were gettin' all red, and every once in a while you'd grab your shirt collar and fan yourself down your front, and I'd look at you and...
MAY	And what?
QUINN	...nothing. Throb. Ten points. (*marking the score*)
MAY	Well, I...I guess I should be flattered
QUINN	What about you? Did you...you know...was there anything about...well, about me that you might've noticed?
MAY	(*putting some tiles down*) Well, Quinn. it's different for me, you know, being a married woman. I don't look at men in that way.
QUINN	Oh, right, right.
MAY	Buns. Nine points.
QUINN	So, does that mean when you get married you don't notice someone who you would've found attractive before? (*putting some tiles down*)
MAY	No, not necessarily. You just don't look at them with any sort of longing that's all.
QUINN	Oh. Lips. Six.
MAY	(*putting some tiles down*) Of course, with Brian leaving, I'm sure the time will come when I will start noticing men, you know, in that way.
QUINN	With longing.
MAY	Right.

QUINN	Right. Well, let's hope it doesn't take you too long. I mean, a good one might come and go and you'll have missed him.
MAY	Well, that's a chance I'll have to take. Mouth. Ten.
QUINN	Mouth? (*looking at her mouth*)
MAY	Mouth. (*staring at his mouth*)
QUINN	Good.

They are very close now.

MAY	Is it getting warm in here?
QUINN	Little bit. Must be the fire.
MAY	There is no fire.
QUINN	Well, not that you can see.
MAY	You know, I think I've had enough Scrabble for one night. (*standing*)
QUINN	Yeah, I'm about spent myself.
MAY	Yes, all of a sudden I'm kind of tired. How about you?
QUINN	Bone weary. (*standing*)
MAY	I guess it's time to go to bed.
QUINN	Yeah.
MAY	Well goodnight then. (*holding her hand out to shake*)
QUINN	(*shaking her hand*) Goodnight.
MAY	See you in the morning.

QUINN   First thing.

MAY   (*still holding QUINN's hand*) Sleep tight.

QUINN   You too.

> *They turn and take one or two steps
> away from each other, QUINN toward
> his room, and MAY toward the stairs,
> then they turn back to each other,
> embrace and kiss passionately. Lights
> down.*
>
> *End Act One, Scene Three.*

Act Two, Scene One

The time is the next morning. As the scene opens, MAY's Little Bo Peep dress is still on the floor where she took it off. We again hear the song "True Love". QUINN enters from the kitchen. He is well-groomed and he wears a nice pair of pants and a shirt and sweater which he's borrowed from MAY's husband. He is carrying a pitcher of orange juice and two glasses on a tray. He moves towards the stairs. MAY enters on the staircase. She is looking much the worse for wear. She is dressed in her housecoat and holds her head as she moves down the stairs.

QUINN   Oh, good morning.

MAY doesn't answer. She moves to the cassette player and turns it off.

MAY   Do you have to play that so loud?

QUINN   I thought you liked loud music in the morning.

MAY   Who told you that? Ronny Hall?

QUINN   Actually, you did. Last night.

MAY	Oh. Last night. Right. Uh...listen, Quinn, I should apologize. I mean, I had quite a bit to drink last night and I probably said a lot of stupid things.
QUINN	You also said I was a great lover.
MAY	(*beat*) Uh-huh. Look, about that whole thing that we...you know, that you and I did.
QUINN	Are you trying to tell me I wasn't?
MAY	Wasn't what?
QUINN	You know? A...uh...
MAY	Oh, no, no. Not at all.
QUINN	Oh, good. Because, you know, I was kind of nervous. I mean, I felt like a ball player coming out of retirement after eight years. You know, like you're not sure if you've still got the stuff, but, then you get that bat in your hands and it all comes back to you.
MAY	(*beat*) I need some coffee. (*moving toward the kitchen*)
QUINN	Sure. (*pulling a slip of paper from his shirt pocket*) Oh, listen, I was just going over this list of things you wanted me to do...
MAY	No, no, no. Please. Coffee first, list later.
QUINN	Whatever you say.
	MAY exits to the kitchen, Off, we hear the crash of pots and pans. MAY enters from kitchen, obviously hurting from a hangover.
QUINN	That was next on the list. Sit down. I'll pour you some orange juice.

MAY sits and QUINN pours juice.

MAY   Please, God, if I ever drink that much again, please take me before morning comes.

QUINN   There you go. (*raising his glass to hers in a toast*) To the flag. (*drinking*) Well?

MAY   Well what?

QUINN   You didn't say what you think. (*holding his arms out so she can look at him*)

MAY   It was nice, Quinn. Very nice. And yes, I did. Two or three times as I recall.

QUINN   No, no, no. I mean the clothes. How do you like the clothes?

MAY   Oh. Oh, very nice.

QUINN   You think so?

MAY   Yes. You look...

QUINN   Like a new man?

MAY   Yes.?

QUINN   It's funny, you know? I almost feel like one. See this? (*holding up glass of juice*) Straight orange juice. No booze. You know why?

MAY   Because I drank it all?

QUINN   No. It's because of what you said last night.

MAY   What, about you being a good lover?

QUINN   No, no — and you said great lover — no, what I was talking about was what you said about me being an example of 'what self-pity can do to a person'.

MAY   Oh, yes. I'm sorry about that.

QUINN   No, you were right. But, in my case, it wasn't
                       self-pity. There's a big difference between feeling
                       sorry for yourself and not feeling a damned thing.
                       What happened to me was I gave up. You see, it
                       seemed that everybody in this town just wanted
                       me to go away because I reminded them of that
                       whole thing with my folks. And so, when they
                       buried my parents, I guess I let them bury me
                       too. I turned into that rube you spoke about. But,
                       being in this house again...I don't know...I
                       remember what it was like. A family lived here.
                       A real family. We weren't bad people. I mean,
                       hell, bad? My mother was the organist at the
                       Church. My father was the Chief of Police. He
                       looked after these people. But, they've forgotten
                       all about that. And why? Because he fell in love
                       with another woman? Is that it? Or...or do they
                       want to forget about it because of the way it all
                       ended up? Maybe they feel responsible somehow,
                       I don't know. But, I don't think they should
                       forget that for all those years, he was a friend of
                       theirs. And my mother and I, we were their
                       friends too. They should remember that. I should
                       make them remember. I don't know how exactly
                       but it won't be by being invisible, and that's
                       what I've been up until now.

MAY   Well, Quinn, I wish you the best of luck.
                       (*getting up and moving toward the stairs*)

QUINN   Where are you going?

MAY   Well, unlike you, I haven't seen the light at the
                       end of the tunnel yet. I've got a house I can't pay
                       for, a business I can't afford to run, and a ten-
                       year-old pick-up truck that I can't afford to put
                       gas in.

QUINN   So, what are you going to do?

MAY   What anyone in my position would do. I'm
                       going back to bed.

QUINN	Now, that's not the answer and you know it. (*grabbing her arm*)
MAY	Let me go. Just lemme sleep for a little while.
QUINN	No.
MAY	Just for a week or two.
QUINN	No. I'll tell you what. We'll help each other. Huh? We'll see each other through the winter.
MAY	Oh, hell. I probably won't even be here past Christmas. I can't afford it.
QUINN	What about the bank? A loan.
MAY	Good luck there. After what happened with Hank last night? And what's this about we? Did I say we were a 'we' last night?
QUINN	No, but...I mean, we were for a while.
MAY	Well, yeah, but that wasn't really being a 'we'. That was just being....you know...
QUINN	Great lovers.
MAY	Right.
QUINN	It's a good jumping off point though, don't you think?
MAY	I'm going back to bed. (*starting for the stairs as QUINN stops her again*)
QUINN	No. No, you're not.
MAY	Look at me. Brian was right. I'm a mess. Even you look better than I do.
QUINN	Oh, come on. You look cute in your bathrobe.
MAY	And my ratty hair?

QUINN	Yes, and your ratty hair.
MAY	Is it really ratty? It is, isn't it?
QUINN	May, some women are attractive no matter what they look like.
MAY	Well, that makes a lot of sense, doesn't it?
QUINN	(*holding her by the arms*) No, May, it's true. Outward appearance doesn't matter sometimes. There are some women, like you, who...who shine out from the inside. It's like they have a beacon for a soul, and they just shine.
MAY	What're you, Neil Diamond?
QUINN	(*pulling her closer*) It's true. And everyone around them wants to get closer...just as close as they can...so they can warm themselves. (*kissing her*)
MAY	(*kissing him for a moment then pulling away*) Quinn...Quinn, please. I know that we were...you know, very close last night for a time, but...
QUINN	Forget about last night. Let's talk about today.
MAY	Quinn, please...
QUINN	No. Now, here's what you're going to do. You're going to go upstairs, put on your best dress, and then you're gonna go to the bank.
MAY	It won't work.
QUINN	It can't hurt to try.
MAY	I want to talk about last night.

There is a knock on the door.

MAY	Oh, what now? You stay there. We have to talk. (*moving to the door, opening to see HANK*) Oh, Hank. Come in. Look, Quinn. It's Hank. From the uh....from the uh...
HANK	Bank.
MAY	The bank. Right. Hank from the bank. Come in, Hank. Come in.

HANK enters, carrying flowers.

HANK	Well, I don't want to intrude.
MAY	Oh, you're not intruding. We were just talking about....baseball.
HANK	Baseball?
MAY	Yes. We just discovered that we're both big baseball fans.
HANK	Really? Well, you know, I swing a pretty mean bat myself.

MAY and QUINN exchange glances.

QUINN	If you'll excuse me, I've got a shelf that needs repairing. (*exiting to the kitchen*)
MAY	Come in, Hank. Come and sit down. (*moving to the table*)
HANK	What happened to him?
MAY	Quinn? Oh, I loaned him some of my husband's clothes. Quite an improvement, isn't it?
HANK	Yes. Not that it would've taken much.
MAY	Speaking of appearances, you'll have to excuse the way I look. I'm afraid I overdid it last night. Went a little crazy.

> *HANK looks at the dress on the floor and picks it up.*

HANK Really?

MAY Oh, let me get that out of your way. (*grabbing the dress and throwing it down the hall towards QUINN's room*) There we go. Please, sit. Can I get you anything? Coffee? Juice?

HANK No. Thank you. I just wanted to bring you these. (*handing MAY the flowers*)

MAY Oh, well, thank you, Hank. They' re lovely.

HANK Well, it's my way of apologizing for my behaviour last night.

MAY Oh, you didn't have to do that.

HANK No, I did. I was out of line and I'm very sorry. I embarrassed myself and embarrassed you, and...

MAY Oh, now stop it. We just had too much to drink last night, that's all.

HANK No, I won't blame the liquor. I knew exactly what I was doing. Exactly. And all those things I said? I meant them, May. Every one.

MAY Even the...pagan stuff?

HANK Especially the pagan stuff. But, I shouldn't have said them. I was just overcome by the romantic setting I guess.

MAY Romantic setting? Hank, we were setting up the Scrabble game. You were dressed in a bunny suit.

HANK You felt it too, didn't you? Well, anyway! I hope you'll forgive me.

MAY Of course I will. In fact, I was coming to see you today to apologize.

HANK	You? What for?
MAY	Well, for hurting your feelings.
HANK	Oh, don't give it another thought. I had it coming.
MAY	No.
HANK	No, I did. I don't know what made me think you'd do something like that on our very first date. I should've waited until the third or fourth date. (*waiting for her to agree, and getting no response*) Fifth or sixth? (*beat*) Until hell freezes over.
MAY	Hank, sometimes it's just not in the cards for a man and a woman.
HANK	You're talking about you and me, right?
MAY	Right. But, there's no reason why we...
HANK	Why we can't be friends?
MAY	Yes.
HANK	Right. Well, that's fine. Friends is good. Friends is nice. In fact, I've remained *friends* with pretty well every woman I've ever gone out with. (*aside*) God, I'm so sick of friends. Well, I'd better get going.
MAY	Oh, Hank, there is one more thing. I've been thinking about what you said about a loan. You know, if I decided that I might need some money to get me through the off season?
HANK	Yes?
MAY	Well, I think I might need some.
HANK	Oh. Alrighty. How much?

They sit at the table.

MAY   Well, I don't know yet. I haven't actually sat down and figured it out, but it would probably be around...

HANK   Thirty-four hundred?

MAY   Around that.

HANK   The amount your husband withdrew from the account.

MAY   Yes.

HANK   Uh-huh. So, does this mean that he's not bringing the money back?

MAY   I'm afraid he's not.

HANK   He's not coming back at all, is he?

MAY   No.

HANK   I see. Another woman, right?

MAY   How did you know?

HANK   Well, Tom and Eunice Miller were out for their midnight stroll last night — they take one every night, helps the circulation in Tom's bad leg — and as they were passing by your door here, they heard someone yelling something about strumpets and lousy sex. Well, after they realized you weren't actually talking about them, they put two and two together and...so is that what it was?

MAY   Yes.

HANK   Ah. Well, that's what Eunice said it must've been. She has a sense about these things. Do you know Eunice at all?

MAY   No.

HANK   Well, they were at the Halloween dance last night. Tom was the cucumber and Eunice was the Nazi. They're good people.

MAY   So, what do you think, Hank?

HANK   Think?

MAY   About the loan.

HANK   Oh, the loan, yes. Well, you'll have to go through the proper channels of course. You can come into the bank today if you like and fill out the necessary forms.

MAY   All right. I can do that.

HANK   Good. And then all we have to do is wait and see if it gets approved. (*standing, getting ready to go*)

MAY   Wait and see? What do you mean wait and see? Aren't you the one who okays it?

HANK   Well, I can make a recommendation, certainly, but the final decision will rest with the loans officer.

MAY   Oh. Who's that?

HANK   Eunice Miller.

MAY   The Nazi. Wonderful. But, you made it sound like there would be no problem. Remember? The bank is there for me? Helping neighbours?

HANK   Absolutely. And I'm sure there'll be no problem.

MAY   Oh. Well, good. Good.

HANK   There is one thing though.

MAY   What?

HANK	And it may have no bearing whatsoever on the outcome of the application, but...
MAY	What? What is it?
HANK	Well, it's Quinn.
MAY	What about him?
HANK	Well, a lot of folks are starting to wonder about...well, quite frankly about the arrangement you two have here.
MAY	Arrangement?
HANK	Now, it's not me. I've told you I'm more mindful of city ways and how relaxed the morals are, but I'm afraid that's not the case with most folks around here.
MAY	Hank, the only arrangement Quinn and I have is a business arrangement. He helps me out with the place and I give him a room.
HANK	I know. I know. But, there are those who look and see a married woman living in this big old house with another man. Him wearing her husband's clothes. Her in her bathrobe. Outerwear strewn about. (*looking at the Scrabble board*)
MAY	Oh, Hank, don't be ridiculous. There is nothing going on here. Nothing! How can you even think that? (*looking at the Scrabble board*)
HANK	(*pointing to the board*) There's no E in horny, by the way. The thing is, May, it looks untoward, and some folks at the bank might feel that by giving you a loan, we'd be condoning a questionable situation. And I'm not sure we can afford that kind of image.
MAY	Image?
HANK	Well, we do have a clientele to think of.

MAY   (*getting angry*) Oh, really? And were you thinking of your clientele last night when you were trying to boink Little Bo Peep?

HANK   Now, that was a different matter altogether.

MAY   Oh, was it now?

HANK   Yes. That's not the same as you carrying on with the likes of Quinn.

MAY   Why you hypocritical bastard.

HANK   Now, there's no need for name-calling.

MAY   You hypocritical little weasel of a bastard. Get out! Get out of my house! And take your flowers with you. (*throwing the flowers at him*)

HANK   (*backing toward the front door*) I should warn you, May, this isn't going to improve your chances for that loan.

MAY   I don't want your loan! I don't want anything from you people. Now, get out!

HANK   May

MAY   Out!

> *HANK exits and MAY closes the door. A moment later HANK opens the door and pokes his head in.*

HANK   One more thing, May. Have you made up your mind yet about the basketball game tonight?

MAY   Out!

> *HANK exits. QUINN enters from the kitchen, having heard everything.*

QUINN   See what I mean? I've got a definite image problem here.

MAY   You heard?

QUINN   Yeah.

MAY   Well, don't pay any attention to him.

QUINN   No, it's okay. I didn't expect them to welcome
               me back to their bosom without a fight. Listen,
               the shelf's all fixed in there. That just leaves the
               back porch on my list here. (*moving toward the
               hall*)

MAY   Quinn? (*moving*) Quinn, wait. He's just jealous
               that's all.

QUINN   Jealous? Jealous of what? Nothin' goin' on here.
               Right?

MAY   And what's that supposed to mean?

QUINN   Nothing. It's like you said. It's a business
               arrangement.

MAY   Oh, no. Oh, no you don't. You're not going to
               make me feel guilty about this.

QUINN   About what?

MAY   About last night.

QUINN   What have you got to feel guilty about?

MAY   About making love with you and then saying
               there's nothing going on here.

QUINN   Well, it's true. Last night was...it was like that
               night at Kelty's bar eight years ago. That's all it
               was.

MAY   What? How can you say that?

QUINN   Well, what was it then? What makes it any more
               than that?

MAY	Me. I make it more. I'm not some insecure female who's angry at her husband because he's spending time with another woman. (*beat*) All right, maybe I am, but that's not why last night happened.
QUINN	Then why did it?
MAY	Because...
QUINN	Because you had too much to drink?
MAY	That was a small contributing factor. That wasn't the main reason.
QUINN	Well, what was it? Pity?
MAY	Oh, don't be an ass!
QUINN	I'm being an ass?
MAY	You're being an ass!
QUINN	Well, let me tell you something, *Mrs. Henning!* You were right. There *is* nothing going on here. The last thing I need is someone like you complicating my life.
MAY	Hah! What's to complicate? You call that a life?
QUINN	Well, it's better than nothing!
MAY	Not by much!
QUINN	Better than spending your life in bed.
MAY	Oh, yeah? Well, I was enjoying myself in bed until I let you in.
QUINN	And what's that supposed to mean?
MAY	It means you need some more batting practice, Slugger! (*moving to the stairs*)

QUINN	Oh, yeah?
MAY	Yeah!
QUINN	Well, that's not what you said last night.
MAY	I was drunk and stupid last night. (*moving up the stairs*)
QUINN	Well, I'm glad to see you're not drunk anymore!
MAY	(*coming back down the stairs*) Oh, so you're saying I'm stupid now?
QUINN	No, ma'am. For all I know, you may have been stupid before too!
MAY	Oh, I was stupid all right. I was stupid to let you stay here in the first place.
QUINN	And I was stupid to accept your invitation.
MAY	Invitation? You begged me to let you stay!
QUINN	I didn't beg.
MAY	Oh, no. Giving me that line about a cold barn and a cow. Please!
QUINN	It was a cold barn, and there was a cow.
MAY	(*skeptical*) Right. And so you came here.
QUINN	That's right. At least it isn't cold here. (*exiting*)
MAY	Oooh!!!

> *MAY storms up the stairs. After a beat she enters again. She is a little remorseful.*

MAY Quinn? I.....

> *MAY sees that QUINN's not there. She comes down the stairs. She wants to make up but decides not to and exits up the stairs again. QUINN enters again feeling a little remorseful also. He moves to the stairs, looks up, and then, changing his mind, exits r. Again.*
>
> *Lights down. End Act Two, Scene One.*

Act Two, Scene Two

> *The time is later that evening. The table
> S.R. is set for a candlelight dinner for
> two. QUINN enters still dressed in
> BRIAN's clothes. He carries his
> overnight bag with him as he moves to
> the front door. He sets the bag down
> near the door. Then he moves and
> admires the table for a moment. MAY
> enters from the kitchen. She has a dress
> on now and she looks great. She carries
> a bottle of wine.*

MAY   Oh, there you are. Will you open this for me,
please? And don't come into the kitchen. It's a
disaster area.

> *MAY hands him the wine and corkscrew
> and heads back to the kitchen.*

QUINN   May?

> *MAY stops.*

What's all this?

MAY   Dinner. I thought we'd celebrate tonight.

QUINN   Celebrate what?

MAY   I don't know. Our first fight. Independence?
Anything.

QUINN   And what's this? (*indicating her dress*)

MAY   What's the matter with it?

QUINN   Nothing. But, it's...it's a dress.

MAY   Very good. Now, open the wine. (*exiting to the kitchen*)

QUINN   But, May, I...

> *After a beat, QUINN sets the bottle on the table, then turns and begins to move upstage. MAY enters carrying a full salad bowl.*

MAY   Where are you going? Open, open.

QUINN   May...

MAY   If it doesn't breathe now it won't be ready for the main course.

> *QUINN comes back and opens the bottle of wine. MAY puts the dish on the table.*

MAY   Do you like lasagna? Don't worry about it. You don't have a choice anyway. It's my best dish. (*fidgeting with the cutlery, rearranging it*) I was going to cook some fresh lobster but the last time I cooked a lobster, I swear I heard the little bugger putting some sort of crustacean curse on me as I dropped him into the pot. All right, Greek salad, rolls...You like feta cheese, don't you?

QUINN   Yeah, but...

MAY   Good. Okay, sit, sit. (*pulling out a chair for him*)

QUINN   May, I can't. (*pushing the chair back in*)

MAY   What do you mean you can't? Sit. (*pulling the chair out again*)

QUINN   No, I can't, really. (*starting to push the chair in again*)

MAY   (*grabbing the chair firmly to prevent him from moving it*) Look, can't you tell when a woman is trying to apologize? I'm sorry, okay? I'm sorry I said there was nothing going on here.

QUINN   Oh, hell. I don't care about that. I mean, I know that nothing could ever happen between you and me.

MAY   Why couldn't it?

QUINN   Well...

MAY   I mean, I'm not saying it could either, of course not, but why couldn't it?

QUINN   Well, I'm not your type.

MAY   How do you know what my type is?

QUINN   It's easy. Your type is a guy with a car phone. A guy who wears slacks instead of pants, ya know? Somebody successful.

MAY   Is that what you think? You really think that?

QUINN   Hey, don't worry about it. You're not my type either.

MAY   What do you mean I'm not your type? What's wrong with me?

QUINN   Nothin's wrong with you. You're just not my type.

MAY   You haven't had a woman in eight years. How can you have a type?

QUINN	I've got a good memory.
MAY	Well, then why did you make love to me if I'm not your type?
QUINN	Well, that was...you know, that was the booze. You'd been drinking, I'd had some.
MAY	Oh? And why did you kiss me this morning?
QUINN	Well, that was the booze too.
MAY	You were drinking straight orange juice.
QUINN	That's right. I was out of my head with sobriety.
MAY	No, I'm sorry. I'm not buying it. I think you were genuinely attracted to me.
QUINN	And I thought you were attracted to me. (*turning and moving*)
MAY	Where are you going?
QUINN	I'm leaving.
MAY	What?
QUINN	I can't stay here anymore.
MAY	Why? I said I was sorry.
QUINN	You've got nothing to be sorry about. Stop apologizing for everything. This has got nothing to do with what's going on between you and me.
MAY	Well, what then? I mean, what is it with you men? I cook you a meal and you leave.
QUINN	May, my being here is only gonna be trouble for you. I mean, with getting that loan and all...
MAY	That's why you're leaving?! Because of that?

QUINN	Yeah...
MAY	Listen, if I think you're trouble, then I'll throw you out myself, okay? But let me make the decision.
QUINN	No, I think it's best all round if I go right now. (*moving to the door*) Oh, I'm gonna have to keep these clothes for a while. I threw my old ones out.
MAY	Quinn, didn't you hear what I just said.
QUINN	May, I'm leaving. That's it, all right. Please. Now, the back porch is all fixed, and you've got enough wood in the shed to last you a couple of months or so. (*picking up his gym bag*) I only wish I could do more for you, May. You've been....well, you've been real good to me. Better than anyone's been in quite a while and I thank you for it. By the way, you look pretty. Real pretty.
MAY	Quinn...

BRIAN enters wearing a sports jacket over a shirt and sweater with casual slacks.

BRIAN	Hello, May. (*looking at QUINN then speaking to MAY*) Am I interrupting?
QUINN	No, I was just leaving. Thanks again. Mrs. Henning. Maybe I'll see you around. (*exiting*)
MAY	Quinn?
BRIAN	Quinn? That was that Quinn fellow. That odd job person?
MAY	That's right.
BRIAN	He looks different. New clothes?

MAY	Yes.
BRIAN	Oh. (*still looking out the door in QUINN's direction*) Salvation Army by the look of it. (*looking at MAY*) You, on the other hand, look terrific.
MAY	(*coldly*) Thank you. (*closing the door and moving down*) So, Brian, what brings you back to this whistle stop.
BRIAN	Well, May, it's kind of urgent actually. (*moving down*) Oh, what's this? Dinner for two. Are you expecting someone?
MAY	Uh...as a matter of fact, yes I am.
BRIAN	Anybody I know.
MAY	No, just a man from town here.
BRIAN	A man? Well. A romantic encounter, is it?
MAY	Possibly.
BRIAN	Uh-huh.
MAY	Well, yes...yes, probably.
BRIAN	Oh. Someone you just met recently, or...
MAY	Fairly recently, yes.
BRIAN	So what's this? First date, second, what?
MAY	I don't remember.
BRIAN	Uh-huh. Well, have you, you know...done the deed yet?
MAY	Well, that's none of your business, now is it?
BRIAN	Just asking.

MAY   Well, what a thing to say. Asking a person something like that. That's extremely personal, Brian. And what do you care if we have or haven't?

BRIAN   I don't.

MAY   Well, we have.

BRIAN   Fine.

MAY   A couple of times in fact.

BRIAN   Good.

MAY   No, it was great.

BRIAN   Well, he must be special. You're even wearing a dress. Boy, you don't waste much time, do you? No, ma'am. No flies on you. Well, anyway, that's too bad. I was kind of hoping I could stay the night.

MAY   Oh?

BRIAN   But, I certainly don't want to get in the way of any tryst you might have planned. (*picking at the salad*)

MAY   And by 'stay the night', what exactly do you mean?

BRIAN   Stay the night. You know? Bed? Some sack time?

MAY   You wish.

BRIAN   What's the matter? Would that be so terrible?

MAY   Oh, Brian, please...

BRIAN   What?

MAY	Look, I know I'm weak, but my God. What happened? Did you get tired of Miss Potato Head? Find out you didn't love her after all? Or did she get tired of you? Huh? That's what happens you know. Her type, they like a man just fine so long as he's married and not a threat to their freedom. Sure, they can see him once, twice, three times a week. A little dinner, a little sex, and no chance of being tied down, unless it's to a headboard for twenty minutes at a time. But, once he leaves the little woman and starts to talk long term, watch out. They're gone before you can say cheap perfume. And what do you do? Back to the wife. She'll take you back, right? Well, not this wife, honey. This wife has moved on. This wife is dust. So, you can just forget about putting in any sack time here, sweet cheeks.
BRIAN	I didn't come here to sleep with you, May.
MAY	No, I'll bet you didn't.
BRIAN	I just thought you could let me have a room.
MAY	(*still doubting him*) A room, right.
BRIAN	Yes, a room. So I wouldn't have to drive all the way back tonight.
MAY	Oh, sure, I'll...back where?
BRIAN	To the city.
MAY	To the...well, what are you here for if it's not...I mean, you said it was urgent.
BRIAN	It is. We're flying down to Barbados next week and I came to pick up my summer clothes.
MAY	Oh.
BRIAN	You didn't really think I came all the way out here to...

MAY   No, of course not. Well, how did I know what
               you came out here for? It could've been for
               anything.

BRIAN   Well, not for that. (*starting to laugh*)

MAY   Well, it could've been. What's so funny?

BRIAN   Oh, May. You know, I think that's why I fell in
               love with you in the first place. You had this raw
               innocence about you.

MAY   Your clothes are upstairs in the front bedroom,
               Brian.

BRIAN   Right. (*moving up the stairs*) Don't get me
               wrong, May. It's not that I wouldn't enjoy it. It's
               just that right now I think it's important for me
               to be faithful.

MAY   Well, better late than never.

BRIAN   May, look...

MAY   Just get the clothes, Brian, all right?!

               BRIAN exits up the stairs

               (*to herself, mocking BRIAN*) We're flying down
               to Barbados. Well, let's hope the Bermuda
               Triangle is more than just a rumour.

                   MAY pours herself a glass of wine.
                   There is a knock on the door.

               (*angry*) Come in!

                   HANK enters.

HANK   May?

MAY   Oh, it's you. Come to foreclose, have you? Well,
               go ahead. Take it. Take the whole damned place.
               You like the mugs? Take em'. Have a ball.

HANK	No, that's not why I've come.
MAY	No? Well, what is it then?
HANK	Well, I was just on my way home from the basketball game and...well, I wanted to say I was sorry about what happened this morning. That was very unprofessional of me. I was letting my personal feelings get in the way of business. That should never have happened. It's unconscionable. The thing of it was, I...I mean, with you and Quinn, it was like Penny Hermitage all over again. You came to the dance with me, but you ended up with him. So, anyway, I apologize, and if you still want that loan, it's yours.
MAY	Do you mean it?
HANK	I'll arrange it first thing Monday morning.
MAY	Well. I don't know what to say. Come here. This deserves a hug.
	HANK and MAY hug. BRIAN enters on the stairs carrying a cardboard box.
BRIAN	(*seeing HANK*) Ah. And this must be your gentleman caller. (*setting the box on the table and moving to HANK*)
MAY	What?
BRIAN	Well, well, well. Nice to meet you. I'm Brian Henning. May's husband?
HANK	Hank Beavis.
	They shake hands.
BRIAN	Hank? Well, how very rural.
MAY	Brian, this...

BRIAN   I've seen you around, haven't I?

HANK   We met actually. When you applied for your mortgage. I work at the bank.

BRIAN   Ooh, a banker. Well, good for you, May.

MAY   No, this...

HANK   And then we met again at the Labour Day barbecue.

BRIAN   Did we? Did we indeed? Well, isn't life strange? One day we're throwing idle chit chat back and forth at a country cook-out, and the next, you're roasting your weenies in my bed.

MAY   Brian!

BRIAN   Oh, May, it's all right. I'm just having a little fun with ol' Hank here. I don't care, Hank. I really don't. You can sleep with May as often as you like.

HANK   (*beat*) Thanks.

BRIAN   And you don't have to worry about being named in the divorce either. (*picking up the box*)

MAY   Divorce?

BRIAN   Well, it's the next logical step, isn't it? Listen, May, you're sure I can't stay? I'll pay you for the room.

MAY   No, I don't think so, Brian. (*putting her arm around HANK's waist*) You probably wouldn't get much sleep anyway. You see, Hank and I, we get kind of loud. Don't we, Hank?

HANK   (*still not quite catching on*) Loud?

BRIAN   Really? You never got loud with me.

MAY	You never found my volume control.
BRIAN	And he has?
MAY	Numerous times.
BRIAN	Well, well done, Hank.
HANK	(*to MAY*) Did I miss something?
MAY	Hank, dinner's almost ready, sweetheart. Why don't you so ahead and start on the salad?
HANK	Dinner?
MAY	Oh, I know you probably want to go upstairs right away, but first things first, okay? There we go. (*pushing him gently toward the table*) He's like an animal sometimes.
BRIAN	Really? You wouldn't know it to look at him.

BRIAN exits .

MAY	Oh, God. God, what's wrong with me? How could I do that? I'm sorry. Hank. It's just that he makes me so mad, with his little girlfriend and his summer clothes. He's so damned smug. He has no consideration for me at all. Just waltzes in here, let's me make a fool of myself and then waltzes out again.
HANK	Well, don't let him. A person can only make a fool out of you if you let him.
MAY	So, what am I supposed to do? Let him think that my life has come to a standstill. Just because he left?
HANK	Has it?
MAY	I don't know. Maybe it has.

HANK	Well, then get it going again. You don't have to pretend for him. You don't have to pretend for anybody. Just be what you really are.
MAY	I'm lonely and miserable.
HANK	Then be lonely and miserable. Be absolutely disconsolate. Be a wretch if that's what you are!
MAY	Is this supposed to help me?
HANK	I don't know. I saw it on Oprah.

BRIAN enters again.

BRIAN	Well, I'm all set. (*to HANK*) Hank, it was a pleasure. You be good to this little lady now. She deserves the very best. (*to MAY*) I'm off, May.
MAY	Brian, I've got something to tell you.
BRIAN	What?
MAY	I was lying.
BRIAN	Lying about what?
MAY	Everything. Hank and I don't have a date tonight. I didn't even know he was coming over. And we haven't slept together either. Not once. And I seriously doubt that we ever will. (*to HANK*) Isn't that right, Hank?

HANK doesn't answer.
Hank?

HANK	Right, right.
MAY	(*to BRIAN*) I didn't put this dress on for him. This dinner isn't for him. In fact, the man I cooked this dinner for walked out. Okay? So, there's no man. There's no one. Just me.

BRIAN	So, what are you saying? Are you saying I can stay over now?
MAY	No, that's not what I'm saying. I'm telling you this because I...
BRIAN	Oh, I get it. I see. May, please, don't do this. It's no use. It's over. And telling me that you've remained faithful, it doesn't change things. You've got to accept that and move on. Now, I really must go. I've got a long drive ahead of me. You take care now, you hear? (*kissing her on the forehead*)
MAY	Brian, wait. One more thing. (*moving toward the kitchen*) Just wait there for just a second. I'll be right back.

> *MAY exits to the kitchen. There is a awkward pause.*

HANK	A little nippy out there tonight, isn't it?
BRIAN	Uh-huh.
HANK	'Course, it is November so I guess we have to expect it. (*beat*) Could be warmer though. Sometimes we get the wind blowing in across the water there and it gets as cold as a witch's heart. (*beat*) Especially that January wind. Brings the snow down from the north? Whew! (*beat*) 'Course we won't have to worry about that 'til...well, 'til January.
BRIAN	(*beat*) So, you're quite the stud, are you?
HANK	(*looking behind him to see if there is a stud there, then back to BRIAN*) I'm sorry?
BRIAN	May can't seem to keep her hands off you.
HANK	Well...
BRIAN	So, how do you do it?

HANK	I beg your pardon?
BRIAN	How do you do it? What's your secret?
HANK	(*beat*) A big carrot.

> *MAY enters from the kitchen carrying two strips of raw bacon in one hand and a raw egg in the other. She moves to BRIAN.*

MAY	Here you are. I wouldn't want you to make that long trip without your bacon and eggs. (*stuffing the bacon then the egg in his shirt pocket*)
BRIAN	What?
MAY	There you go.
BRIAN	May, this isn't funny.
MAY	(*patting the pocket firmly then kissing him on the forehead*) You take care now, you hear? Don't make me worry about you.

> *MAY ushers BRIAN out the door quickly and closes it behind him, then moves to the table.*

	Hank, this is your lucky night. I am going to give you the best meal you've ever had.
HANK	Oh, that's very nice of you, May, but I really can't stay.
MAY	Why not?
HANK	(*beat*) I'm leaving.
MAY	Here we go again.
HANK	I only stopped by to tell you about your loan and to bring this over. (*pulling a medallion from his jacket*)

MAY	What's this? Oh, it's your medal from the basketball team.
HANK	No. No, actually it's...it's Quinn's. I...uh... didn't get one. I guess they forgot. (*handing it to MAY*)
MAY	Oh, Hank...
HANK	Ah, it's okay. I mean, I wasn't really part of the team I guess. You know, I was just the towel boy....So anyway, I think I'm going to take that job at the bigger branch. I mean, I'll only be a couple of hours away by car, so I can drive down to see Mother whenever I want and...well, I just think it's time. So, that's why I can't stay for dinner. I have to go home and break the news to Mother. I don't want her finding out from someone else.
MAY	Who else knows?
HANK	Well, I kinda mentioned it to Ronny Hall. (*moving to the door*)
MAY	Hank, are you sure about this?
HANK	Positive.
MAY	And you won't miss this town?
HANK	I don't know. Do you think the town'll miss me?
MAY	I think a lot of us will.
HANK	Good-bye, May.
	HANK exits. MAY moves to the table and sits. She takes a sip of wine. QUINN enters from the kitchen.
MAY	Quinn?
QUINN	So how'd it go with your husband?

MAY	Oh, it went fine.
QUINN	Uh-huh. I noticed he was loading up his clothes there.
MAY	You were watching?
QUINN	Well, yeah, you know, I waited around just out of curiosity.
MAY	Uh-huh. Well, he took his clothes all right.
QUINN	So, you didn't take him back?
MAY	No. No, I didn't.
QUINN	Ah. Came begging did he?
MAY	Well, I wouldn't exactly say he was begging. (*beat*) Grovelling is more like it
QUINN	Well, good for you. You stood your ground. You see? You're getting strong. Of course, being on your own, that's gonna be the real test.
MAY	Oh, I think I'll be okay.
QUINN	You think so?
MAY	Yeah. I mean, turns out I've been alone for a long time anyway. I just didn't know it.
QUINN	So, that means what? You don't need anybody anymore?
MAY	That's right.
QUINN	Well, good. Good. Looks like you've won the war then.
MAY	Of course, that doesn't mean that I won't ever want someone. There's a big difference between need and want.

QUINN	Uh-huh. Well, if you ever want somebody, word around town is that Ronny Hall's got a big crush on you.
MAY	(*smiling*) Really?
QUINN	Oh, big crush, yes.
MAY	Well, my, my.
QUINN	Oh, I should warn you though, your husband'll probably be back this way soon.
MAY	Oh, I don't think so.
QUINN	(*reaching into the bag he's carrying*) No, I think he will. Just as soon as he misses his car phone. (*pulling the phone from the bag and giving it to MAY*) You told me it was yours so I figured you should have it.
MAY	Thank you. Oh, I've got something for you too. (*getting the medal and giving to QUINN*) Hank brought this over for you.
QUINN	(*reading the medal*) District Champions. Nineteen Seventy-One. Daniel Quinn. Well, I'll be damned.
MAY	Why didn't you go tonight?
QUINN	Well, I...I don't know. I figured they'd probably forgotten.
MAY	Well, they didn't.
QUINN	No. How bout' that?
MAY	I think this calls for a toast. (*handing QUINN a glass of wine picking up one for herself*) To...uh...to the team of '71.
QUINN	To yesterday's heroes. It was fun while it lasted boys.

MAY	And to your trip back to a better place.
QUINN	Same to you.
	They drink.
	Well, I'd better get going. I figure if I sweet talk Frank Tucker's cow maybe she'll let me come back.
MAY	Oh, you're not going back to that barn, are you?
QUINN	Well, just until I can find something better.
MAY	You can stay here if you like. I've got lots of room.
QUINN	No, I don't think that'd be a good idea.
MAY	Well, if it's the loan you're worried about, Hank says I'll probably get it now.
QUINN	No, no, it's not the loan.
MAY	Oh? Well what is it then?
QUINN	Well, to be perfectly honest, it's you.
MAY	Oh. I see. You can't stay in the same house with me, is that it?
QUINN	That's it.
MAY	You dislike me that much?
QUINN	No, not exactly.
MAY	Well, what is it?

QUINN   Well, it's just that if I was staying here, I don't think I could resist the temptation to come to your room late at night and make passionate, burning, heart-pounding love with you until dawn.

MAY   Oh. Well, we certainly don't want that hanging over our heads.

HANK   No. So, I really think it'd be better if I just left. I need a little time anyway, you know?

MAY   Oh, sure. Sure. I guess we both do.

QUINN   I mean, you know what they say about time.

MAY   It flies.

QUINN   No.

MAY   It marches on?

QUINN   It heals all wounds.

MAY   Oh, right, right. Well, maybe it's better that we take some time then.

QUINN   Right.

MAY   Right. And I mean, you can always come back and finish later.

QUINN   Finish? Finish what?

MAY   Well, your work. The work you were supposed to do for me in return for your room and board.

QUINN   But, I did finish it.

MAY   You did? Well, what happened with the back door?

QUINN   What about the back door?

MAY	It doesn't close properly. Never has.
QUINN	I didn't notice that.
MAY	Why do you think it's so drafty in here?
QUINN	I didn't think it was.
MAY	Sure, you're used to living in a barn.
QUINN	Well, why wasn't it on the list?
MAY	What, do I have to write everything down for you? You haven't got any initiative?
QUINN	Sure I do. I just didn't know anything was wrong with the damn door.
MAY	Well, don't worry about it. I can fix it.
QUINN	No, I'll fix it.
MAY	No, you're in a hurry. Go on.
QUINN	No, if it was part of the deal we had then I'll fix it. I don't like to leave a job unfinished. Probably just needs to be shaved down a bit anyway.
MAY	You think that's all it needs?
QUINN	Sure. Take me five minutes.
MAY	Oh. All right. Good. Of course, you never know. Maybe it needs more shaving down than you think.
QUINN	Well, so it takes me a half hour then. Big deal.
MAY	(*moving closer to him*) Or maybe shaving it down won't do it at all. Maybe it'll have to be replaced altogether.
QUINN	Well, then I'll replace it.

MAY   And how long will that take?

QUINN   Well...that depends. I mean, I'd have to send away for a new door. That'd take some time.

MAY   How much time?

QUINN   A week. Maybe two. (*beat*) And new doors are funny. You know, sometimes they don't fit right in with the old frame.

They move closer together.

MAY   What happens then?

QUINN   Well, then you gotta replace the frame too.

They kiss.

Aw, hell, I may have to knock down the whole damn wall.

They kiss and light go down. The End.